"I say the measure of a man is not how tall you stand, how wealthy or intelligent you are. 'Cause I found out the measure of a man God knows and understands for He looks inside to the bottom of your heart, and what's in the heart defines the measure of a man."

—The Measure of a Man
by 4 Him

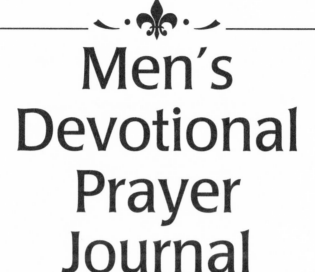

Men's
Devotional
Prayer
Journal

*"The effective, fervent prayer of
a righteous man avails much."*
JAMES 5:16

WORD PUBLISHING
Dallas•London•Vancouver•Melbourne

PRESENTED TO:

Dad

FROM

Bryan & Michele

DATE

December 25, 1996

~· CONTENTS ·~

⌣· FOREWORD ·⌣

I BELIEVE WE MAY BE ON THE THRESHOLD of one of the greatest
revivals the world has ever seen. Already, we see signs of the coming revival
in the men's movement sweeping America, and in renewed interest in prayer
by men. This *Men's Devotional Prayer Journal* is just one more evidence that
the Holy Spirit is doing a fresh work in our time. One thing is certain:
No great revival has ever occurred that was not preceded by a widespread
concert of prayer on the part of godly men (and women). In the words of
James:

> "*. . . The effective, fervent prayer of a righteous man avails much.*"
> *(James 5:16b)*

There is much said and written about the effective executive and the
effective pastor, but not nearly enough about the effective man or woman of
prayer. The point about *effectiveness* that needs to be born in mind is that it is
always a matter of accomplishing what you set out to do, of seeing results
from your efforts. In the case of prayer, it is a matter of receiving answers to
your petitions. Is that not why we pray, in addition to the joy of being in the
presence of the Lord? Of course it is. After all, our God is a prayer-hearing
and prayer-answering God.

The key phrase in the text just quoted from James is "a righteous
man." The effective, fervent prayer of a righteous man avails much, but the
fervent prayer of an unrighteous man avails *nothing*, is not effective at all. As
Isaiah reminds us:

> "*But your iniquities have separated you from your God; and your
> sins have hidden His face from you, so that He will not hear.*"
> *(Isa. 59:2)*

Put simply, personal righteousness is a condition for effective praying. If our
lives are not clean, God will not listen.

The Holy Spirit never brings revival without bringing conviction of sin. It is His role to bring such conviction, as Jesus told His disciples:

"And when He has come, He will convict the world of sin, and of righteousness, and of judgment." (John 16:8)

Once the Holy Spirit points out areas of our lives with which we need to deal by repentance and change, we must respond in obedience. When we do, God will send revival. He promised to do so long ago in a covenant He made with Solomon:

"If My people who are called by My name will humble themselves, and pray and seek My face, and turn from their wicked ways, then I will hear from heaven, and will forgive their sin and heal their land." (2 Chron. 7:14)

James repeats this covenant in a different form as a condition for effective prayer:

"Confess your trespasses to one another, and pray for one another, that you may be healed. . . ." (James 5:16a)

While James in this context is referring to physical healing, the same condition applies to prayer for the healing of our land.

I would hasten to point out that keeping vows is another condition for effective praying:

"Offer to God thanksgiving, and pay your vows to the Most High. Call upon Me in the day of trouble; I will deliver you, and you shall glorify Me." (Ps. 50:14–15)

Here we have a promise from God that if we call upon Him in the day of trouble, He will hear us and deliver us—a promise contingent upon keeping our vows to Him.

The Scripture also speaks directly to men about the correlation between their treatment of their wives and the effectiveness of their prayers:

"Husbands, likewise, dwell with them with understanding, giving honor to the wife, as to the weaker vessel, and as being heirs together of the grace of life, that your prayers may not be hindered." (1 Pet. 3:7)

In this text, we read that husbands are to treat their wives honorably, as the weaker vessel, and to do it lovingly as God has commanded us. Why? Lest our prayers be hindered! There are vast numbers of people who have offered prayers that are never answered because of the treatment of their spouse; because they are not living with their spouse the way God has commanded them to. In the case of husbands, it is because they are not loving their wives as Christ loved the church (Eph. 5 :25). Here, then, is a third condition for effective praying.

There are other conditions for answered prayer as well, such as praying in faith (Heb. 11:6), obeying Christ's commandments (1 John 3:22), and praying according to the revealed will of God (1 John 5:14). These conditions are referred to in the helps to prayer provided in this Journal. We need to fulfill all of the conditions of effective prayer if we are to receive answers to our petitions.

My friends, if we would be godly men, if we would be spiritual men, we *must* give ourselves to prayer. This is of tremendous importance. We cannot grow in spirit unless we are men of prayer. Oh, that God would deliver us from little, or weak, or unfervent prayers! The most important time that we can spend in this world is the time we spend with God in prayer.

I have shared with you the major conditions of effective prayer and have pleaded with you to be men of prayer. But you may still be asking yourselves whether there are good and sufficient reasons for paying the price required to become effective men of prayer. You have busy lives and many demands on your time, and you will spend time and expend effort only on those things that pay dividends in your lives. You can be moved by emotional appeals, but your intellect requires reasons before you will commit yourself to wrestling with God in prayer the way Jacob did (Gen. 32:24).

Why should we pray? First of all, if we do not, then God, our heavenly Father, and Christ, the heavenly Bridegroom, are defrauded of their right of communion with us. What would any husband think if his wife never had time to talk to him, to commune with him, to share herself with him? I am sure that he would notice and grow tired of the strange silence that filled the house. So it is if we, the bride of the heavenly Bridegroom, do not share ourselves in communion and prayer with Him, we are defrauding Christ of His rights in a bride.

Second, we should pray because if we do not our own lives are greatly impoverished. "Thou hast made us for Thyself," said St. Augustine, "and our hearts are restless till they rest in Thee." There is no doubt that the restlessness, the stress, the anxiety, the worry, and the fear that wreak such havoc in so many lives today would melt away before the rising sun of prayer and flee, like so many bats out of a cave, from the prayer closet of a praying saint.

We are personally enriched by prayer. The joy and love, the warmth, the meaning and significance of life that come from prayer cannot be obtained anywhere else. Only God can provide for our hearts. The most beautiful scene upon which I can gaze will not beautify my heart. The loveliest wind that blows will not cleanse my soul. Only the work of Christ's Spirit can do those things through prayer. How many things God desires for us that we miss by not praying. I assure you that your life will be infinitely more blessed if you pray. *More things are wrought by prayer than this world dreams of.*

Third, we ought to pray because the Kingdom of God needs to grow and expand and spread its beneficent influence over the hearts and minds of men throughout the world. We are called to be intercessors, to go beyond the grammar school of prayer where we simply ask for various things for ourselves (although there is nothing wrong with that). We are to pray for others; we are to join the soldiers of Christ who are working for the Kingdom of God and are laboring to win the souls of men to Christ. If we do not become prayer warriors, we cannot expect to see a great harvest of souls or the revival God wants to bring in our midst.

For the reasons I have given, and many others besides, I would urge you to give yourself unto prayer, effective prayer, that God would bless you and that you would be a blessing to this world as you call down upon its multiple needs the very power of God's Spirit. Be a man of prayer! God will bless your heart . . . God will bless your home . . . God will bless your church . . . God will bless your nation . . . God will bless this world.

D. James Kennedy, Ph.D.
Senior Minister
Coral Ridge Presbyterian Church
Fort Lauderdale, Florida

IMPORTANCE OF A DEVOTIONAL PRAYER JOURNAL

THE WAY CHRISTIANS RECEIVE *POWER* for daily living, and the means through which God releases His *grace* into the world, is believing *prayer*. As Christians, we are "the salt of the earth" and "the light of the world" (Matthew 5:13–14). We cannot give light to a dark world or be used by God as a preservative in a decadent society unless we are plugged into the *power* source, God Himself, through believing *prayer*.

Many times Christians in our society dash off quickie prayers as they fall asleep at night or just before they need God's help for some specific task. We have allowed ourselves to become anemic spiritually because we regard everything else in our hurry-up lives as more urgent and more important than our devotional time with the Lord.

What are we saying by this behavior? Are we telling God we are too busy to spend quality time with Him? Are we saying we do not *need* what He has provided in the way of spiritual resources, that we do not *need* to hear Him speak to us through His Word, or that we do not *need* to talk to Him in prayer? Surely, we would never consciously express such thoughts. Perhaps we should remind ourselves of the words of the Lord as He taught His disciples about their total dependence on Him:

> *"I am the vine, you are the branches. He who abides in Me, and I in him, bears much fruit; for without Me you can do nothing."* (John 15:5)

Notice the benefit of drawing from our *power* source, the Lord Jesus Christ: we become fruitful in our work and witness for Christ!

To receive this benefit, we must take time each day to be alone with the Lord. When we want to accomplish a certain number of things in a given day, we write up a "to do" list and check it off when we have completed the things we wanted to get done. A *devotional prayer journal* serves a similar purpose, by outlining day by day and week by week a program of Bible reading, meditation, Scripture memorization, and prayer. If it is all laid out for us, we are less likely to forget our devotions or omit vital parts of our prayer life.

Because it is important for us to *respond* to what God is teaching us, and to have a permanent *record* of lessons and blessings, places are provided to write down applications of Scripture and results of prayer. Near the beginning of most of his letters, Paul indicated the prayers he was making on behalf of the churches (see Romans 1:8–10). He did this to communicate both *care* and *encouragement*. When we record the results of our prayers, we are reminded how much God *cares* for us. At the same time, we are *encouraged* to persevere in our worship of the Lord.

THE SPECIFIC MEANING OF PRAYER

❦

PRAYER IS ASKING GOD PERSISTENTLY in faith for the right thing with the right motive. Let us reflect on this definition of prayer:

1. *Asking God.* Even though God knows what we need before we ask Him (see Matthew 6:8), He still bids us to ask (see Matthew 7:7). Prayer is a declaration of dependence on God, an acknowledgment that everything good in our lives is given to us by Him (see James 1:17).

2. *Persistently.* On more than one occasion, Jesus taught His disciples that we are never to give up in bringing our needs to God (see Luke 11:5–8; 18:1–5). This is sometimes called *importunate prayer.* It means we are to keep on asking, seeking, and knocking until God answers (see Luke 11:9).

3. *In Faith.* Jesus also taught His disciples that if we ask God for something, we must believe He will answer. If we believe without doubting, we will receive what we ask for (see Matthew 21:21–22; Mark 11:23). James says that to do otherwise is to be like the waves tossed by the wind, to be double-minded (James 1:6–8).

4. *For the Right Thing.* The Lord's Prayer teaches us that it is always right to pray that God be glorified, that His will be done, that our real needs be met, and that we be kept from evil (see Matthew 6:9–13). Beyond these things, it is always right to pray for what God has revealed to be His will in the Bible (see 1 John 5:14–15), to believe that He will answer if we do His revealed will (see 1 John 3:22).

5. *With the Right Motive.* The right motive in prayer is to seek the honor and glory of the Lord Jesus Christ in what we ask (see John 12:28; 17:1). When our prayers are "gimme" prayers, when we seek to satisfy our own desires instead of God's, we know at the outset we will not receive what we ask for (see James 4:3).

As believers, we sometimes wonder if we are praying for the right thing with the right motive. If we have been conscientious in following the principles just outlined, we can stop worrying. We have an intercessor dwelling within, the Holy Spirit, who passes our requests through the grid of God's will, and the Father receives our requests through the mind of the Spirit (see Romans 8:27). Finally, we have an intercessor dwelling with the Father, the Lord Jesus Christ, who constantly pleads our case (see Romans 8:34; Hebrews 7:25; 1 John 2:1).

PURPOSE OF MEDITATION

READING THE BIBLE MECHANICALLY, just sitting down and putting in time, is not listening to God as He applies the truth of His Word to our lives. If we do not discern the will of God as we read His Word, we will not know what to pray for as we ought. The same Holy Spirit who dwells within us and intercedes for us when we pray is the One who will enable us to understand the truth of Scripture and who will apply it to our lives. As Jesus told His disciples:

> *"But the Helper, the Holy Spirit, whom the Father will send in My name, He will teach you all things, and bring to your remembrance all things that I said to you." (John 14:26)*

When we turn the Word of God over and over in our minds and hearts, when we think about what it says, when we ponder the things the Holy Spirit is trying to teach us, when we reflect on its application to our lives, that is called *meditation*.

The apostle Paul, in the same passage in which he urges us to bring everything to the Lord in prayer (see Philippians 4:6), also calls upon us to focus our thinking on the eternal truths found in God's Word:

> *"Finally, brethren, whatever things are true, whatever things are noble, whatever things are just, whatever things are pure, whatever things are lovely, whatever things are of good report, if there is any virtue and if there is anything praiseworthy—meditate on these things." (Philippians 4:8)*

Whatever we make the focus of our thinking soon becomes the basis of our behavior, as the psalmist suggests:

"I will meditate on Your precepts, and contemplate Your ways."
(Psalm 119:15)

The one who ponders the truth of God's Word and acts upon it is the one the Lord promises to bless (see Joshua 1:8; Psalm 1:1–3).

Another way to give the Holy Spirit an opportunity to teach us and lead us is to *memorize* passages of Scripture that we have already read and meditated upon (see Psalm 119:11). Later, when God wants to deal with us or give us a word to share with others, the Holy Spirit will bring to our remembrance what we have hidden in our hearts. That is why a memory verse is suggested for each of the weekly Bible readings in this devotional prayer journal.

WHY WE PRAY THE SCRIPTURES AND CLAIM THEM FOR OURSELVES

THE PRIMARY REASON WHY IT IS especially powerful to take the truth the Holy Spirit has taught us as we read, meditate upon it, memorize Scripture, and then pray it back to the Lord during our devotions is that God promises to answer prayers based on His *revealed will!*:

> *"Now this is the confidence that we have in Him, that if we ask anything according to His will, He hears us. And if we know that He hears us, whatever we ask, we know that we have the petitions that we have asked of Him." (1 John 5:14–15)*

God gives us an advance guarantee of positive answers to any prayers based on His known will as revealed in His Word. That is one reason the Lord Jesus taught His disciples to pray that the heavenly Father's will be done on earth as it is in heaven (see Matthew 6:10).

One historical example that bears repeating is based on the commandment with promise that God gives His Son in the Psalms:

> *"Ask of Me, and I will give You the nations for Your inheritance, and the ends of the earth for Your possession." (Psalm 2:8)*

Taking this to be God's will in his life as well, the great reformer, John Knox, prayed:

> *"Give me Scotland, or I die!"*

Knox's passionate prayer was marvelously answered and the Presbyterian Church was born.

In addition to specific commandments, the entire Bible is full of *promises* that we may claim for ourselves. Both the Old and New Testaments make it clear that we can trust God to keep His promises because He is absolutely trustworthy and cannot lie (see Numbers 23:19; Titus 1:2).

God promises to:

1. Give us eternal life if we trust Christ as Savior (John 1:12; 3:16),

2. Forgive our sins if we confess and forsake them (1 John 1:9),

3. Heal those for whom we pray in faith, in accordance with His will (James 5:14–15),

4. Meet all of our needs out of His riches in glory (Philippians 4:19),

5. Raise us up at the last day (John 6:39, 40, 44, 54).

What great and precious promises we have to claim (see 2 Peter 1:4)!

How to Make
Personal Application
and Record Personal Insights

ONE APPROACH TO MAKING PERSONAL application of the Scripture is to ask ourselves a series of questions as we read and meditate on the Word of God. At the same time, we should pray that the Holy Spirit would open our minds to understand what we are reading, would teach us truths on which we can meditate, would convict us of changes we need to make in our lives, and would incline our wills to obey the will of God. We should ask such questions as:

1. What does God want me to *know* in this passage; what *truths* is He teaching me?

2. What does God want me to *be* or *become* in light of these truths?

3. What does God want me to *think* or *feel* as a result of this passage?

4. What does God want me to *do*; how does He want me to *act* as a consequence of commandments in this passage?

5. What promises does God want me to *claim*; how does He want me to *pray* based on this passage?

Sometimes, the Holy Spirit will cause the lesson He wants to teach us virtually to leap off the page and enter our hearts and minds like a bolt of lightning! At other times, because of the circumstances of our lives, we will smile or break out laughing because the passage we are reading so perfectly fits our situation.

The lines printed on each page of this devotional prayer journal are provided so we may record personal insights, as we meditate, and the applications based on those insights. They may also be used to write specific prayer requests, and later the results of those requests. Suppose we have just read (and perhaps memorized) Philippians 4:19:

"And my God shall supply all your need according to His riches in glory by Christ Jesus."

Using the questions outlined above, I should meditate on this passage and ask the Holy Spirit to apply it to my life:

MEDITATION

When God says "all" my need, He means all! If His riches are "by Christ Jesus," I know Jesus has all power in heaven and earth!

APPLICATION

Instead of worrying about my tax bill, I should go to the Lord and ask His help in meeting this need.

I might then record a specific prayer request as a follow-up to the application:

PRAYER REQUEST

Lord, the tax bill needs to be paid, but I don't know where it's going to come from.

PRAYER RESULT

Praise you, Lord! I didn't expect this insurance check for another month. What timing!

By reviewing our prayer requests from time to time, we have an instant dated prayer list. We are also able to be reminded of God's past faithfulness and to be encouraged about the future, no matter what challenges we face.

DIFFERENT TYPES AND TOPICS OF PRAYER

UNLESS WE CONSCIOUSLY include the different types of prayer (confession, thanksgiving, praise, supplication, intercession) as well as the different topics of prayer (for government leaders, family members, friends, healing, guidance, revival) in our devotional prayer times, we may omit certain vital aspects of our prayer life or find our prayers reduced to personal petitions at times of extremity. To help us remember these various types and topics of prayer, and to provide models we can use to get started each time, the following pages will be devoted to such models. Even the apostle Paul had to remind Timothy to maintain a balance in the prayer life of the church:

> *"Therefore I exhort first of all that supplications, prayers, intercessions, and giving of thanks be made for all men, for kings and all who are in authority, that we may lead a quiet and peaceable life in all godliness and reverence." (1 Timothy 2:1–2)*

In other places, Paul would add poignantly: "And for me, . . ." (see Ephesians 6:19)

⌣· CONFESSION ·⌣

There is a beautiful scene following the Lord's Supper that illustrates the basic reason why we need to confess our sins daily. Jesus got up, laid aside His outer garments, and tied a towel around His waist. He then knelt down and proceeded to wash the disciples' feet, drying them with the towel. When He came to Peter, Peter protested and then asked Jesus to wash his hands and head as well (acknowledging his sinfulness by this request). Jesus' response to Peter sets forth the condition of a believer who has sinned as well as the remedy for this condition:

"Jesus said to him, 'He who is bathed needs only to wash his feet, but is completely clean; and you are clean, but not all of you.'"
(John 13:10)

A believer has already been cleansed once completely when he or she first comes to Christ in repentance and receives Him as Savior (1 John 1:9). Thereafter, when we sin, it is like an ancient traveler whose feet are dirty from walking on dusty roads in open sandals. When the traveler comes in off the road, he just needs to have his feet washed to be completely clean again. When we confess the particular sins we have committed since the last time we confessed, the Lord declares us forgiven and completely cleansed from all unrighteousness.

The effects of unconfessed and unforsaken sin for the believer are far more serious than unwashed feet! Since God made us to have fellowship with Him, any sin in the life of a child of God has the effect of breaking fellowship between that person and his or her heavenly Father. Essentially, this was the experience Jesus had on the cross as He bore our sins. That was why He cried out:

"My God, My God, why have You forsaken Me?" (Matthew 27:46)

His relationship with the Father was unbroken; He was still the son of God. But the communication lines were down since God is "of purer eyes than to behold evil" (Habakkuk 1:13). Our relationship with God remains secure, even when we sin. But we are no longer on speaking terms with Him and are not at that point usable in His service. How important it is to keep short accounts with God!

The Holy Spirit will show us those things in our lives that are displeasing to God, if we listen to Him as He applies God's Word to our hearts:

"And when He has come, He will convict the world of sin, and of righteousness, and of judgment." (John 16:8)

The following passages deal with confession and are followed by sample prayers to help us get started in this area of prayer:

Scripture: "You ask and do not receive, because you ask amiss, that you may spend it on your pleasures." (James 4:3)

Prayer: Please forgive me for my self-centered prayers . . .

Scripture: "We have sinned and committed iniquity, we have done wickedly and rebelled, even by departing from Your precepts and Your judgments."(Daniel 9:5)

Prayer: Father, have mercy on America! . . .

Scripture: "For we do not have a High Priest who cannot sympathize with our weaknesses, but was in all points tempted as we are, yet without sin."(Hebrews 4:15)

Prayer: Lord Jesus, it is comforting to know You faced the same kind of temptation . . .

Scripture: "All we like sheep have gone astray; we have turned, everyone, to his own way; and the LORD has laid on Him the iniquity of us all." (Isaiah 53:6)

Prayer: When I consider what I've done, I feel so stupid sometimes . . .

Scripture: "No temptation has overtaken you except such as is common to man. . . ."(1 Corinthians 10:13)

Prayer: I should have been warned by the failure of others . . .

Scripture: "Therefore, to him who knows to do good and does not do it, to him it is sin."(James 4:17)

Prayer: It was within my power to help them, but I didn't . . .

⌁· CONFESSION ·⌁

Date	Name	Prayer Request	Prayer Result

~·CONFESSION·~

Date	Name	Prayer Request	Prayer Result

⌣· CONFESSION ·⌣

Date	Name	Prayer Request	Prayer Result

⌣·CONFESSION·⌣

Date	Name	Prayer Request	Prayer Result

~·CONFESSION·~

Date	Name	Prayer Request	Prayer Result

~·CONFESSION·~

Date	Name	Prayer Request	Prayer Result

⌣· THANKSGIVING ·⌣

Everything worthwhile in life, including life itself, is a gift from God:

"Every good gift and every perfect gift is from above, and comes down from the Father of lights, with whom there is no variation or shadow of turning." (James 1:17)

When someone receives a gift, the most natural thing—indeed the expected thing—is to express gratitude to the giver. Perhaps that is why the Lord expressed surprise when only one out of ten lepers whom He had cleansed bothered to return to give thanks, and that one was a Samaritan:

"So Jesus answered and said, 'Were there not ten cleansed? But where are the nine? Were there not any found who returned to give glory to God except this foreigner?'" (Luke 17:17–18)

One sign of fallenness, of human beings in rebellion against God, is ingratitude. This was true at the beginning when human beings rejected the knowledge they had of the true God for that which was false:

"Because, although they knew God, they did not glorify Him as God, nor were thankful. . . ." (Romans 1:21)

This will be true at the end when self-centered human beings regard themselves as self-sufficient:

"For men will be lovers of themselves, lovers of money, boasters, proud, blasphemers, disobedient to parents, unthankful, unholy. . . ." (2 Timothy 3:2)

The opposite is true of a child of God. Believers know where their blessings come from! In fact, when any really good thing happens to a Christian, the spontaneous response of his or her heart is to exult:

"Thank you, Lord!"

The greatest tragedy for an unbeliever is to experience something special and have no one to thank.

Perhaps the most distinctive thing about a believer's gratitude is that it is possible to exult even under terrible circumstances. Paul and Silas sang in prison (Acts 16:25), and Job blessed God after everything was taken away (Job 1:21). Paul summed it up well when he said:

"In everything give thanks; for this is the will of God in Christ Jesus for you." (1 Thessalonians 5:18)

Scripture: "The LORD will give strength to His people; the LORD will bless His people with peace." (Psalm 29:11)

Prayer: Thank You for giving me peace in the middle of the storm . . .

Scripture: "Bless the LORD, O my soul, and forget not all His benefits." (Psalm 103:2)

Prayer: Where do I begin to thank You for all You have done for me? . . .

Scripture: "But He was wounded for our transgressions, He was bruised for our iniquities; the chastisement for our peace was upon Him, and by His stripes we are healed." (Isaiah 53:5)

Prayer: Thank You for healing my soul . . .

Scripture: "It is good for me that I have been afflicted, that I may learn your statutes." (Psalm 119:71)

Prayer: Thank You for the lessons of Your discipline . . .

Scripture: "Giving thanks always for all things to God the Father in the name of our Lord Jesus Christ." (Ephesians 5:20)

Prayer: I can thank You even for this because I come to You in Jesus' name . . .

~·Thanksgiving·~

Date	Name	Prayer Request	Prayer Result

ᵔ·THANKSGIVING·ᵔ

Date	Name	Prayer Request	Prayer Result

Date	Name	Prayer Request	Prayer Result

~·THANKSGIVING·~

Date	Name	Prayer Request	Prayer Result

Date	Name	Prayer Request	Prayer Result

~·Thanksgiving·~

Date	Name	Prayer Request	Prayer Result

⁓· PRAISE ·⁓

Praise is pure worship. Whereas thanksgiving is the believer's response to God for what He has *done*, praise is the believer's response to God for who He *is*. The two are closely related in many of the psalms:

> *"Enter into His gates with thanksgiving, and into His courts with praise. Be thankful to Him, and bless His name." (Psalm 100:4)*

The angels of heaven likewise pour out their praise before God:

> *"All the angels stood around the throne and the elders and the four living creatures, and fell on their faces before the throne and worshiped God, saying: 'Amen! Blessing and glory and wisdom, thanksgiving and honor and power and might, be to our God forever and ever. Amen.'" (Revelation 7:11–12)*

The prayer the Lord taught His disciples begins and ends with praise:

> *"Our Father in heaven, Hallowed be Your name. . . . For Yours is the kingdom and the power and the glory forever. Amen." (Matthew 6:9, 13)*

The Westminister Shorter Catechism states it succinctly:

> *"The chief end of man is to glorify God and to enjoy Him forever."*

Praise is the creature's response to the Creator. God alone is worthy of adoration. To worship anything or anyone else is idolatry. Again, such idolatry is another mark of fallen, rebellious creatures:

> *"Who exchanged the truth of God for the lie, and worshiped and served the creature rather than the Creator, who is blessed forever. Amen." (Romans 1:25)*

It is significant that Satan's fall resulted from trying to displace the Creator as the object of worship. It is also significant that the devil tried to tempt

Jesus to worship him, to which Jesus responded:

> *"Away with you, Satan! For it is written, 'You shall worship the* LORD *your God, and Him only you shall serve.'" (Matthew 4:10)*

The irony is that we never rise so high as when we are on our face before the Lord. Worship lifts and ennobles us, because it demonstrates that we are made in the image of God—made for worship and a personal relationship with our Creator. By contrast, nothing debases us so much as when we fail to honor the one true God.

Scripture: "For in him we live, and move and have our being, . . ." (Acts 17:28)

Prayer: I worship You as my creator and sustainer . . .

Scripture: "And you will seek Me and find Me, when you search for Me with all your heart." (Jeremiah 29:13)

Prayer: O Lord, I adore You more than life itself . . .

Scripture: "My soul waits for the Lord more than those who watch for the morning. . . ." (Psalm 130:6)

Prayer: O Lord, I could not wait to have my devotions this morning! . . .

Scripture: "But you, when you pray, go into your room, and when you have shut your door, pray to your Father who is in the secret place. . . ." (Matthew 6:6)

Prayer: Lord, it is good to be alone with You . . .

Scripture: "He has put a new song in my mouth—Praise to our God. . . ." (Psalm 40:3)

Prayer: You alone make me break out into songs of praise . . .

⌣ᐧ PRAISE ᐧ⌣

Date	Name	Prayer Request	Prayer Result

⊱· PRAISE ·⊰

Date	Name	Prayer Request	Prayer Result

~·PRAISE·~

Date	Name	Prayer Request	Prayer Result

⤖ · PRAISE · ⤘

Date	Name	Prayer Request	Prayer Result

⌁· PRAISE ·⌁

Date	Name	Prayer Request	Prayer Result

⌁· PRAISE ·⌁

Date	Name	Prayer Request	Prayer Result

⌒· SUPPLICATION ·⌒

Earlier, a definition of prayer was offered that begins:

"Prayer is asking God persistently . . ."

This definition relates more closely to supplication than to any other type of prayer. As Paul urges:

"Be anxious for nothing, but in everything by prayer and supplication, with thanksgiving, let your requests be made known to God." *(Philippians 4:6)*

Supplication is asking with a sense of urgency; it amounts to begging or beseeching. When we come to God with our petitions, it should never be casually or indifferently. Our whole heart and soul should be poured out before the Lord in earnest prayer.

In a sense, everything we ask God for could be considered supplication, and that is the use of the term in the acrostic ACTS. (Adoration, Confession, Thanksgiving, Supplication). Specifically, it includes all personal petitions, all requests to meet personal needs. It is with this large category of prayer in mind that the Lord teaches His disciples to pray:

"Give us this day our daily bread." (Matthew 6:11)

God wants to be involved in the everyday details of our lives. He wants us to come to Him with everything. Why? Because He loves us and delights to demonstrate His love in supplying our every need (see Philippians 4:19; 1 Peter 5:7).

Why do we not come to the Lord with all of our burdens and needs? There are two primary reasons: (1) we do not really want God's will in every situation (we have a better idea!); and (2) we do not really believe God loves us and has our best interests at heart. In the Sermon on the Mount, the Lord Jesus Christ deals with both reasons (or rather, rationalizations).

On the first account, Jesus places a petition for the will of God to be done before the petition for God to meet our daily needs:

> *"Your kingdom come. Your will be done on earth as it is in heaven."*
> *(Matthew 6:10)*

In the second case, Jesus shames His disciples by pointing to God's care for birds and plants and then asking why they do not believe God would care for them (Matthew 6:26, 30). He concludes by saying (really, commanding) that pursuing God's will ensures God's provision:

> *"But seek first the kingdom of God and His righteousness, and all these things shall be added to you." (Matthew 6:33)*

Scripture: "Ask, and it will be given to you; seek, and you will find; knock, and it will be opened to you." (Matthew 7:7)

Prayer: Lord, I'm asking . . .

Scripture: "I have been young, and now am old; yet I have not seen the righteous forsaken, nor his descendants begging bread." (Psalm 37:25)

Prayer: O Father, I have lost my job and need to feed my family . . .

Scripture: "And when they had prayed, the place where they were assembled together was shaken; and they were all filled with the Holy Spirit. . . ." (Acts 4:31)

Prayer: Father, send a Holy Ghost revival to our church! . . .

Scripture: "And when He had sent the multitudes away, He went up on the mountain by Himself to pray. . . ." (Matthew 14:23)

Prayer: The world crowds in, and I need a touch from You . . .

Scripture: "But you, beloved, building yourselves up on your most holy faith, praying in the Holy Spirit." (Jude 20)

Prayer: Holy Spirit, make up what is lacking in my prayer . . .

⁓· SUPPLICATION ·⁓

Date	Name	Prayer Request	Prayer Result

∽·Supplication·∽

Date	Name	Prayer Request	Prayer Result

~·SUPPLICATION·~

Date	Name	Prayer Request	Prayer Result

∽·SUPPLICATION·∽

Date	Name	Prayer Request	Prayer Result

~·Supplication·~

Date	Name	Prayer Request	Prayer Result

∽·Supplication·∽

Date	Name	Prayer Request	Prayer Result

⌣· INTERCESSION ·⌣

A special form of prayer or supplication is prayer on behalf of others. Such prayer is called *intercession*. Aside from pure worship (praise or adoration) of God Himself, there is no nobler type of prayer than to intercede before God on behalf of the needs of others. In the Old Testament, this was a special responsibility of prophets. Even when Israel sinned against God by asking for a king, Samuel did not abandon his role as an intercessor for the nation:

> *"Moreover, as for me, far be it from me that I should sin against the* LORD *in ceasing to pray for you. . . ." (1 Samuel 12:23)*

Later on, when Israel faced extinction as a nation, God saw there were no faithful prophets interceding for His people:

> *"He saw that there was no man, and wondered that there was no intercessor. . . ." (Isaiah 59:16)*

In the New Testament, the responsibility for intercessory prayer is extended to all believers:

> *"Therefore I exhort first of all that supplications, prayers, intercessions, and giving of thanks be made for all men." (1 Timothy 2:1)*

Over and over again in his letters, Paul shares with the churches that he is praying for them:

> *"[I] do not cease to give thanks for you, making mention of you in my prayers." (Ephesians 1:16)*

Having said this, we need to examine our commitment in saying to others, "I'm praying for you." We must faithfully intercede for them, and not just express polite words of concern. They are counting on us!

For the Christian, the most significant intercessory prayer that goes on is the ministry performed on our behalf by the Holy Spirit and the Lord Jesus Christ. In the case of the Holy Spirit, we are told:

"Likewise the Spirit also helps in our weaknesses. For we do not know what we should pray for as we ought, but the Spirit Himself makes intercession for us with groanings which cannot be uttered."(Romans 8:26)

In addition, the Lord Jesus is "even at the right hand of God, who also makes intercession for us" (Romans 8:34). We count on Their intercession; others count on us.

Scripture: "Therefore I exhort first of all that supplications, prayers, intercessions, and giving of thanks be made for all men." (1 Timothy 2:1)

Prayer: Lord, You know who is weighing heavily on my heart right now . . .

Scripture: "Peter was therefore kept in prison, but constant prayer was offered to God for him by the church." (Acts 12:5)

Prayer: Lord, please protect . . .

Scripture: "For I was hungry and you gave Me no food; I was thirsty and you gave Me no drink." (Matthew 25:42)

Prayer: Father, give me compassion for the starving of this world . . .

Scripture: "Brethren, pray for us." (1 Thessalonians 5:25)

Prayer: Father, I pray you will take away the suffering of . . .

Scripture: "Praying always . . . in the Spirit, . . . for all the saints—and for me. . . ." (Ephesians 6:18,19)

Prayer: Father, give our pastor boldness to proclaim the gospel on Sunday . . .

~·INTERCESSION·~

Date	Name	Prayer Request	Prayer Result

~·INTERCESSION·~

Date	Name	Prayer Request	Prayer Result

Date	Name	Prayer Request	Prayer Result

~·Intercession·~

Date	Name	Prayer Request	Prayer Result

⌁· INTERCESSION ·⌁

Date	Name	Prayer Request	Prayer Result

⌁· INTERCESSION ·⌁

Date	Name	Prayer Request	Prayer Result

SPECIFIC PRAYERS

NOT ONLY ARE THERE SPECIFIC TYPES of prayer we should incorporate into our devotions, but there are specific topics of prayer—matters for which and persons for whom we should be praying on a regular basis. They include the fruit of the Spirit (love, joy, peace, etc.) and specific issues and needs—temptation, comfort, healing, etc. They also include specific individuals: spouse, parents, children, political leaders, etc.

The main reason we should pray for these various topics is that we are commanded to do so. Even in the case of the fruit of the Spirit, God commands us to exhibit these character traits. We all face temptation on a daily basis, and this was one topic Jesus included in the model prayer He taught His disciples:

"And do not lead us into temptation, but deliver us from the evil."
(Matthew 6:13)

Bereavement is another universal human experience, and we are to "weep with those who weep" (Romans 12:15). As we comfort others, we know we have the Comforter Himself dwelling within us (John 14:16–17). Illness is still another occasion for us to minister to one another. Again, we are commanded to pray for healing and health (James 5:16). A catastrophic illness, the loss of a job, the general economy—all of these things can throw our budgets into a tailspin. God wants us to trust Him and come to Him to meet our financial needs, and He will (Philippians 4:19). Finally, we are commanded in the Great Commission to go into all the world and reach the lost for Christ (Matthew 28:19–20). In all of these areas, God wants us to pray specifically. If we do not, we will not receive specific answers:

"You do not have because you do not ask." (James 4:2)

~·LOVE·~

Scripture: "A new commandment I give to you, that you love one another; as I have loved you, that you also love one another." (John 13:34)

Prayer: Help me to show love to others by serving them, . . .

Scripture: "Love suffers long and is kind; love does not envy; love does not parade itself, is not puffed up." (1 Corinthians 13:4)

Prayer: I confess that my expressions of love have been far too selfish and self-seeking . . .

Scripture: "In this is love, not that we loved God, but that He loved us and sent His Son to be the propitiation for our sins." (1 John 4:10)

Prayer: Father, I praise You for sending Jesus to die for my sins . . .

Scripture: "You shall love your neighbor as yourself." (Matthew 19:19)

Prayer: Forgive me, Lord. I've lived next door to . . . all these years and have not witnessed to them as I should . . .

Scripture: "But I say to you who hear: Love your enemies, do good to those who hate you." (Luke 6:27)

Prayer: I have been so bitter against . . . Show me something concrete I can do to bless him/her . . .

Scripture: "For the love of Christ compels us, because we judge thus: that if One died for all, then all died." (2 Corinthians 5:14)

Prayer: If You loved me enough to die for me, how can I do less than live for You? . . .

⌣· SPECIFIC PRAYERS: LOVE ·⌣

Date	Prayer Request	Date Answered

❧ SPECIFIC PRAYERS: LOVE ❧

Date	Prayer Request	Date Answered

⌁· JOY ·⌁

Scripture: "These things I have spoken to you, that My joy may remain in you, and that your joy may be full." (John 15:11)

Prayer: I thank you for sharing Your joy with me through Your Word . . .

Scripture: "Rejoice in the Lord always. Again I will say, rejoice!" (Philippians 4:4)

Prayer: No matter what the circumstances, You give me cause for joy . . .

Scripture: "My brethren, count it all joy when you fall into various trials." (James 1:2)

Prayer: Lord, help me to rejoice just in knowing that You are using these trials to strengthen my faith . . .

Scripture: "[Jesus] whom having not seen you love. Though now you do not see Him, yet believing, you rejoice with joy inexpressible and full of glory." (1 Peter 1:8)

Prayer: When I remember the day I first trusted in You, my heart is filled to overflowing with the joy I felt then . . .

Scripture: "Looking unto Jesus, the author and finisher of our faith, who for the joy that was set before Him endured the cross. . . ." (Hebrews 12:2)

Prayer: To think that the joy of my salvation was enough for You to be willing to go to the cross! . . .

Scripture: "You will show me the path of life; in Your presence is fullness of joy; at Your right hand are pleasures forevermore." (Psalm 16:11)

Prayer: This world has nothing to compare with the joy of being in Your presence. It's a taste of heaven right here and now . . .

⌁· SPECIFIC PRAYERS: JOY ·⌁

Date	Prayer Request	Date Answered

◟·ᴛSPECIFIC Pʀᴀʏᴇʀs: Jᴏʏ ·◞

Date	Prayer Request	Date Answered

⌣·Peace·⌣

Scripture: "Peace I leave with you, My peace I give to you; not as the world gives do I give to you. Let not your heart be troubled, neither let it be afraid." (John 14:27)

Prayer: Please forgive me for being so anxious instead of claiming Your promise of peace . . .

Scripture: "For He Himself is our peace, who has made both one, and has broken down the middle wall of separation." (Ephesians 2:14)

Prayer: Thank you, Lord, for making me Your friend when I was Your enemy . . .

Scripture: "If it is possible, as much as depends on you, live peaceably with all men." (Romans 12:18)

Prayer: Father, may I be a peacemaker and not a troublemaker . . .

Scripture: "And the peace of God, which surpasses all understanding, will guard your hearts and minds through Christ Jesus." (Philippians 4:7)

Prayer: Lord, I thank You for listening while I poured out my heart. I feel such a peace, and the fear is gone . . .

Scripture: "The things which you learned and received and heard and saw in me, these do, and the God of peace will be with you." (Philippians 4:9)

Prayer: Now I understand. You bring peace to me when I am obedient to You . . .

ᕦ· SPECIFIC PRAYERS: PEACE ·ᕤ

Date	Prayer Request	Date Answered

~· SPECIFIC PRAYERS: PEACE ·~

Date	Prayer Request	Date Answered

✎· TEMPTATION ·✎

Scripture: "No temptation has overtaken you except such as is common to man; but God is faithful, who will not allow you to be tempted beyond what you are able, but with the temptation will also make the way of escape, that you may be able to bear it." (1 Corinthians 10:13)

Prayer: Lord, I confess I have persisted in my sin even when You have made a way of escape . . .

Scripture: "For we do not have a High Priest who cannot sympathize with our weaknesses, but was in all points tempted as we are, yet without sin." (Hebrews 4:15)

Prayer: How thankful I am that You know what I am struggling with, and that because of You I do not have to be defeated . . .

Scripture: "Therefore we also, since we are surrounded by so great a cloud of witnesses, let us lay aside every weight, and the sin which so easily ensnares us. . . ." (Hebrews 12:1)

Prayer: Lord, when I am tempted, remind me of how many people are looking to my example, . . .

Scripture: "Do not love the world or the things in the world. If anyone loves the world, the love of the Father is not in him." (1 John 2:15)

Prayer: I have to admit it. This temptation's allure shows me that at times I love the world more than I love You . . .

Scripture: "But each one is tempted when he is drawn away by his own desires and enticed." (James 1:14)

Prayer: I can't point my finger anywhere else. My own heart is corrupt . . .

Date	Prayer Request	Date Answered

∽· Specific Prayers: Temptation ·∽

Date	Prayer Request	Date Answered

⌣ · COMFORT · ⌣

Scripture: "In My Father's house are many mansions; if it were not so, I would have told you. I go to prepare a place for you." (John 14:2)

Prayer: Lord Jesus, I am overwhelmed to think You are not only preparing a home for Your children in heaven but a specific place of service . . .

Scripture: "Jesus said to her, 'I am the resurrection and the life. He who believes in Me, though he may die, he shall live.'" (John 11:25)

Prayer: Thank You, Lord, for the assurance that because You have risen from the dead, we too shall be resurrected at the last day . . .

Scripture: "And God will wipe away every tear from their eyes; there shall be no more death, nor sorrow, nor crying. There shall be no more pain, for the former things have passed away." (Revelation 21:4)

Prayer: What a joy to know that our loved ones' suffering is over forever! . . .

Scripture: "Jesus wept." (John 11:35)

Prayer: Lord, I know You can feel my pain . . .

Scripture: "But I do not want you to be ignorant, brethren, concerning those who have fallen asleep, lest you sorrow as others who have no hope." (1 Thessalonians 4:13)

Prayer: Thank You, Lord, for the promise that we will see our loved ones again . . .

Scripture: "[Jesus Christ] who died for us, that whether we wake or sleep, we should live together with Him." (1 Thessalonians 5:10)

Prayer: What a thought! To live forever with Jesus! . . .

⌣· SPECIFIC PRAYERS: COMFORT ·⌣

Date	Prayer Request	Date Answered

⌣· SPECIFIC PRAYERS: COMFORT ·⌣

Date	Prayer Request	Date Answered

✎· HEALING ·✎

Scripture: "Pray for one another, that you may be healed. The effective, fervent prayer of a righteous man avails much." (James 5:16)

Prayer: In obedience to Your command, I ask for Your healing touch upon . . .

Scripture: "Bless the LORD, O my soul, and forget not all His benefits; . . . who heals all your diseases." (Psalm 103:2–3)

Prayer: Thank You, Lord, for guiding the doctor's hands . . .

Scripture: ". . . I was sick and you visited Me. . . ." (Matthew 25:36)

Prayer: Now I know the true significance of making those hospital visits . . .

Scripture: "And He said to me, 'My grace is sufficient for you, for My strength is made perfect in weakness.' Therefore most gladly I will rather boast in my infirmities, that the power of Christ may rest upon me." (2 Corinthians 12:9)

Prayer: Whether You choose to heal me or not, I want everyone to see Your strength in my life . . .

Scripture: "Is anyone among you sick? Let him call for the elders of the church, and let them pray over him. . . ." (James 5:14)

Prayer: I've been putting it off, but I'm going to call the pastor and ask for prayer . . .

Scripture: "I said, 'LORD, be merciful to me; Heal my soul, for I have sinned against You.'" (Psalm 41:4)

Prayer: O Lord, heal my sin-sick soul . . .

Date	Prayer Request	Date Answered

~· SPECIFIC PRAYERS: HEALING ·~

Date	Prayer Request	Date Answered

⌁· FINANCIAL NEEDS ·⌁

Scripture: "The blessing of the LORD makes one rich, and He adds no sorrow with it." (Proverbs 10:22)

Prayer: O Lord, You are the source of every material blessing; I need not feel guilty for what You place in my hands . . .

Scripture: "And you shall remember the LORD your God, for it is He who gives you power to get wealth. . . ." (Deuteronomy 8:18)

Prayer: Father, please forgive me for taking the credit for what You have enabled me to earn . . .

Scripture: "Command those who are rich in this present age not to be haughty, nor to trust in uncertain riches but in the living God, who gives us richly all things to enjoy." (1 Timothy 6:17)

Prayer: Lord, help me to remember that "In God We Trust" is not just a motto on our coins . . .

Scripture: "And my God shall supply all your need according to His riches in glory by Christ Jesus." (Philippians 4:19)

Prayer: Father, You know my financial needs right now, and You have promised to meet them . . .

Scripture: "And God is able to make all grace abound toward you, that you, always having all sufficiency in all things, may have an abundance for every good work." (2 Corinthians 9:8)

Prayer: How wonderful to know that You will always provide enough for me to be able to give to Your work and to meet my needs . . .

~· SPECIFIC PRAYERS: FINANCIAL NEEDS ·~

Date	Prayer Request	Date Answered

~· SPECIFIC PRAYERS: FINANCIAL NEEDS ·~

Date	Prayer Request	Date Answered

⁓ · THE UNSAVED · ⁓

Scripture: "Go therefore and make disciples of all the nations, baptizing them in the name of the Father and of the Son and of the Holy Spirit." (Matthew 28:19)

Prayer: Here I am, Lord; send me . . .

Scripture: "For 'whoever calls on the name of the LORD shall be saved.'" (Romans 10:13)

Prayer: Help me to remember that people need to hear about Jesus . . .

Scripture: "But you shall receive power when the Holy Spirit has come upon you; and you shall be witnesses to Me. . . ." (Acts 1:8)

Prayer: Give me a holy boldness in witnessing . . .

Scripture: "For the Son of Man has come to seek and to save that which was lost." (Luke 19:10)

Prayer: If it was Jesus' purpose to reach the lost, then it is mine too . . .

Scripture: "And you He made alive, who were dead in trespasses and sins." (Ephesians 2:1)

Prayer: May I never forget I was once lost . . .

Scripture: "I say to you that likewise there will be more joy in heaven over one sinner who repents. . . ." (Luke 15:7)

Prayer: To think you and the angels throw a party in heaven every time someone accepts Christ!

❦· SPECIFIC PRAYERS: THE UNSAVED ·❧

Date	Prayer Request	Date Answered

Date	Prayer Request	Date Answered

WEEKLY DEVOTIONS

❦

WE APPROACH THE BIBLE as we do no other book. The Bible is God's inspired, inerrant Word. Everything it affirms is true and relevant to our lives. Our attitude as we prepare ourselves to study the Scripture should be one of expectancy and excitement:

> *"Your words were found, and I ate them, and Your word was to me the joy and rejoicing of my heart. . . ." (Jeremiah 15:16)*

The more time we spend in the Word, the more we come to love it and the more it comes to fill our minds and hearts:

> *"Oh, how I love your law! It is my meditation all the day."*
> *(Psalm 119:97)*

We should come to be known individually and collectively as people of the Book.

There are many helps to Bible study and many good Bible teachers. But when it comes to a devotional study of the Word of God, we have one Helper and Teacher who excels them all—the Holy Spirit:

> *"But the Helper, the Holy Spirit, whom the Father will send in My name, He will teach you all things, and bring to your remembrance all things that I said to you." (John 14:26)*

What the Holy Spirit inspired in the writers of Scripture was truth from beginning to end, and what He teaches us is truth and is about the One who is the Truth:

"However, when He, the Spirit of truth, has come, He will guide you into all truth. . . . He will glorify Me, for He will take of what is Mine and declare it to you." (John 16:13–14)

Christ is the grand subject of Scripture, and since Christ is "the same yesterday, today, and forever" (Hebrews 13:8), we should expect the message of the Bible to be consistent throughout. The truth is the truth and is the same for everyone. While applications may vary according to the circumstances of our lives and what God is trying to teach us individually, the truth will not.

While most devotionals just leap off from some text, the devotionals in this journal do not. They provide the reader with a minicommentary on the whole New Testament as they highlight the high points from each week's readings. Complementary Old Testament readings are suggested that further illuminate the daily New Testament readings.

As we meditate upon the daily readings from the Old and New Testaments, we should remember that the Scripture has different functions and these functions are reflected in metaphors used by the Bible to describe itself:

Life The words of Scripture produce eternal life in the first place (1 Peter 1:23); they purify and mature our Christian lives in the second place (Ephesians 5:26; 1 Peter 2:2).

Light The words of the Bible give us understanding of the truth (Psalm 119:130); they also illuminate the path of life by teaching us how to live (Psalm 119:105).

Mirror The Word of God shows us ourselves as we really are; but we are to act on what we see and not forget the images God shows us (James 1:23, 24).

Sword The Word of God is called "the sword of the Spirit" (Ephesians 6:17) and is the one offensive piece of the Christian's armor; God also uses it to bare our spirit before Him (Hebrews 4:12, 13).

Bread	Scripture feeds our souls, nourishes our spiritual lives, as bread feeds our bodies (Deuteronomy 8:3; Matthew 4:4); Christ calls Himself the bread of heaven, which we must eat to live (John 6:51, 58, 63).
Fire	Like a fire, God's Word consumes whatever is false or evil (Jeremiah 5:14); the Holy Spirit causes the truth of Scripture to burn within our hearts (Luke 24:32).
Hammer	The power of the Word of God to humble and convict of sin may be compared to a hammer breaking rocks apart (Jeremiah 23:29); Scripture is profitable for reproof and correction (2 Timothy 3:16).

We can expect the Bible to have all of these functions and more in our lives. A devotional study of the Word of God is anything but dull!

∽· DEVOTIONAL ·∽

THE MIRACLE OF JESUS' BIRTH, the wonder of His miracles, the power of His preaching—all of these together argue for His uniqueness as the Son of God. They also make His commands to let our light shine (Matthew 5:16f) and to exceed the self-righteousness of the Pharisees (5:20) the revealed will of God for godly living. Jesus' moral teachings went deeper and further than the hypocritical legalists of His day. They combine the standard of God's perfection (5:48) with the compassion of His loving heart (5:44), a perfect balance for living.

NEW TESTAMENT	OLD TESTAMENT
Monday. Matthew 1:1–25	Isaiah 7:10–14; Genesis 17:1–8
MEDITATION:	APPLICATION:
Tuesday. Matthew 2:1–23	Psalm 57:1–11
MEDITATION:	APPLICATION:

Wednesday. Matthew 3:1–4:11

MEDITATION: _____

_____

_____

_____

_____

Psalm 34:1–14

APPLICATION: _____

_____

_____

_____

_____

Thursday. Matthew 4:12–5:12

MEDITATION: _____

_____

_____

_____

_____

Genesis 12:1–4; Isaiah 6:1–8

APPLICATION: _____

_____

_____

_____

_____

Friday. Matthew 5:13–37

MEDITATION: _____

_____

_____

_____

_____

Psalm 89:11–15; 97:10–11; 18:28

APPLICATION: _____

_____

_____

_____

_____

Weekend. Matthew 5:38–6:15

MEDITATION: _____

_____

_____

_____

_____

Psalm 25:1–18

APPLICATION: _____

_____

_____

_____

_____

MEMORY VERSE: Let your light so shine before men, that they may see your good works, and glorify your Father in heaven.

Matthew 5:16

⌁ DEVOTIONAL ⌁

JESUS ESTABLISHED THE RIGHT PRIORITIES for His church:
seeking (Matthew 6:33ff) and doing (7:21) the will of God; seeing a lost
world (8:11) in need of forgiveness (9:6); and answering God's call to enter
the harvest as colaborers with Christ (9:37–38). We will suffer persecution
as Christians in this world (10:22), but the Lord encourages us by telling
us of the Holy Spirit's help (10:20) and of the Father's power (10:28). Let us
ask Him to show us His plan for a dying world, and then get in on it!

NEW TESTAMENT	OLD TESTAMENT
Monday. Matthew 6:16–7:6	Nehemiah 9:1–3; Joel 2:12–13
MEDITATION: _____	APPLICATION: _____
_____	_____
_____	_____
_____	_____
Tuesday. Matthew 7:7–8:4	Psalm 1:1–3; 37:23, 24
MEDITATION: _____	APPLICATION: _____
_____	_____
_____	_____
_____	_____

Wednesday. Matthew 8:5–27

MEDITATION: _____

_____

_____

_____

_____

Psalm 104:1–9, 27–33

APPLICATION: _____

_____

_____

_____

_____

Thursday. Matthew 8:28–9:17

MEDITATION: _____

_____

_____

_____

_____

Psalm 32:1–7; 103:8–13

APPLICATION: _____

_____

_____

_____

_____

Friday. Matthew 9:18–10:10

MEDITATION: _____

_____

_____

_____

_____

Psalm 103:1–5; Ezekiel 34:11–16

APPLICATION: _____

_____

_____

_____

_____

Weekend. Matthew 10:11–40

MEDITATION: _____

_____

_____

_____

_____

Psalm 119:41–46; Jeremiah 20:7–9

APPLICATION: _____

_____

_____

_____

_____

MEMORY VERSE: But seek first the kingdom of God and His righteousness, and all these things shall be added to you.

Matthew 6:33

~· DEVOTIONAL ·~

SPIRITUAL BLINDNESS IS AN AWFUL THING. It led the people of Jesus' day to ascribe the ministry of John the Baptist (Matthew 11:18ff) and the miracles of Jesus (12:24) to the devil. It also accounts for why Jesus taught in parables (13:13). The Holy Spirit opens our eyes to understand God's Word (13:11, 23) and our hearts to receive Christ (12:18–21). God's judgment on those who have rejected Christ is also an awful thing, as the parables of the wheat and the tares (13:41–42) and of the fishing net (13:49–50) illustrate.

NEW TESTAMENT	OLD TESTAMENT
Monday. Matthew 10:41–11:24	Proverbs 1:22–31; Malachi 3:1
MEDITATION:	APPLICATION:
Tuesday. Matthew 11:25–12:21	Deuteronomy 10:12–13, 16, 20–21
MEDITATION:	APPLICATION:

Wednesday. Matthew 12:22–45
MEDITATION: _____

Proverbs 10:20–21; 15:3–4, 26
APPLICATION: _____

Thursday. Matthew 12:46–13:17
MEDITATION: _____

Psalm 119:97–106; Ezekiel 12:1–2
APPLICATION: _____

Friday. Matthew 13:18–43
MEDITATION: _____

Deuteronomy 11:18–19
APPLICATION: _____

Weekend. Matthew 13:44–14:12
MEDITATION: _____

Isaiah 9:6–7; Psalm 96:10–13
APPLICATION: _____

MEMORY VERSE: Come to Me, all you who labor and are heavy laden, and I will give you rest.

Matthew 11:28

⌁· DEVOTIONAL ·⌁

EVEN THOUGH JESUS FED two multitudes to satisfy the hunger of their stomachs (Matthew 14:19ff; 15:36), He was far more interested in the condition of their hearts (15:18). He condemned the external religiosity of the Jewish leaders of His day (16:12), and He commended Peter's confession of faith (16:16–18). To be His disciples, we must humble ourselves (16:24) and have the faith of a child (18:3). In our relationships with one another, we must be redemptive (18:15) and forgiving (18:35). Has Christ become Lord of our hearts and our relationships?

NEW TESTAMENT	OLD TESTAMENT
Monday. Matthew 14:13–36	Psalm 111:1–5; 116:1–9
MEDITATION:	APPLICATION:
Tuesday. Matthew 15:1–31	Proverbs 26:24–26; 30:11–13
MEDITATION:	APPLICATION:

Wednesday. Matthew 15:32–16:20
MEDITATION: _____
_____
_____
_____
_____

Numbers 11:21–23, 31–32
APPLICATION: _____
_____
_____
_____
_____

Thursday. Matthew 16:21–17:13
MEDITATION: _____
_____
_____
_____
_____

Psalm 62:11–12; Isaiah 53:6–10
APPLICATION: _____
_____
_____
_____
_____

Friday. Matthew 17:14–18:9
MEDITATION: _____
_____
_____
_____
_____

Psalm 138:1–6; Proverbs 29:23
APPLICATION: _____
_____
_____
_____
_____

Weekend. Matthew 18:10–35
MEDITATION: _____
_____
_____
_____
_____

Ezekiel 18:21–23; Psalm 51:1–11
APPLICATION: _____
_____
_____
_____
_____

MEMORY VERSE: Then Jesus said to His disciples, "If anyone desires to come after Me, let him deny himself, and take up his cross, and follow Me."
Matthew 16:24

⁓· Devotional ·⁓

HOW PEOPLE RESPOND TO JESUS determines their eternal destiny. The rich young man turned away sorrowful because of his possessions (Matthew 19:22ff). The disciples forsook all and were blessed (19:28). The mother of James and John sought prominence for her sons and was corrected (20:23). The crowd who accepted Him cried Hosanna (21:9), and the Jewish leaders who rejected Him were angry (21:15). Jesus becomes either the cornerstone or the crushing stone (21:44). The key to people's response is whether they accept or reject the truth of Scripture (22:29). What is our response?

New Testament	Old Testament
Monday. Matthew 19:1–26	Malachi 2:13–16; Genesis 2:19–24
MEDITATION: _____	APPLICATION: _____
_____	_____
_____	_____
_____	_____
Tuesday. Matthew 19:27–20:19	1 Samuel 2:2–10
MEDITATION: _____	APPLICATION: _____
_____	_____
_____	_____
_____	_____

Wednesday. Matthew 20:20–21:11

MEDITATION: _____

_____

_____

_____

_____

Psalm 95:1–3; 118:24–27

APPLICATION: _____

_____

_____

_____

_____

Thursday. Matthew 21:12–32

MEDITATION: _____

_____

_____

_____

_____

Psalm 26:8; Jeremiah 7:10–14

APPLICATION: _____

_____

_____

_____

_____

Friday. Matthew 21:33–22:14

MEDITATION: _____

_____

_____

_____

_____

Isaiah 56:3–5; Psalm 103:15–22

APPLICATION: _____

_____

_____

_____

_____

Weekend. Matthew 22:15–40

MEDITATION: _____

_____

_____

_____

_____

Deuteronomy 6:4–9; 7:9–11

APPLICATION: _____

_____

_____

_____

_____

MEMORY VERSE: So the last will be first, and the first last. For many are called, but few chosen.

Matthew 20:16

⌐ DEVOTIONAL ⌐

JESUS' TEACHING ABOUT HIS SECOND COMING was meant to do two things: to encourage His own to finish His work of proclaiming the gospel to all peoples (Matthew 24:14ff), and to exhort us to be ready whenever He returns (24:44). For when the judgment comes, He will examine our lives to see if we have been faithful to use the gifts He has given us in His service (25:21, 23). We will be held accountable for the light we have. Judas's betrayal was with knowledge (26:2). How much more accountable will we be with all the light we have? Are we ready for His return?

NEW TESTAMENT	OLD TESTAMENT
Monday. Matthew 22:41–23:22	Ezekiel 13:8–16
MEDITATION: _____	APPLICATION: _____
_____	_____
_____	_____
_____	_____
Tuesday. Matthew 23:23–24:8	Jeremiah 2:30, 34–35
MEDITATION: _____	APPLICATION: _____
_____	_____
_____	_____
_____	_____

Wednesday. Matthew 24:9–35

MEDITATION: _____

_____

_____

_____

_____

Daniel 7:13–14; Isaiah 13:9–10

APPLICATION: _____

_____

_____

_____

_____

Thursday. Matthew 24:36–25:13

MEDITATION: _____

_____

_____

_____

_____

Malachi 3:1–5, 14–18

APPLICATION: _____

_____

_____

_____

_____

Friday. Matthew 25:14–40

MEDITATION: _____

_____

_____

_____

_____

Psalm 41:1–3; 112:5–9

APPLICATION: _____

_____

_____

_____

_____

Weekend. Matthew 25:41–26:19

MEDITATION: _____

_____

_____

_____

_____

Judges 13:15–23; Genesis 8:18–21

APPLICATION: _____

_____

_____

_____

_____

MEMORY VERSE: And this gospel of the kingdom will be preached in all the world as a witness to all the nations, and then the end will come.

Matthew 24:14

◦ DEVOTIONAL ◦

THE EVENTS THAT TRANSPIRED at the end of Jesus' earthly ministry, from the betrayal (Matthew 26:1–3ff), to the mock trial (26:59–68), to Pilate's final decision to hand Jesus over for crucifixion (27:24–26), to the details of His death on the cross (27:35), to His burial (28:6), all happened according to God's plan and scriptural prophecy. Jesus did not have His life taken away; He gave it willingly for us (26:39). After His resurrection, He gave us the Great Commission (28:19–20), along with His promise never to leave us or forsake us (28:20).

NEW TESTAMENT	OLD TESTAMENT
Monday. Matthew 26:20–46	Psalm 73:1–5; Zechariah 13:7–9
MEDITATION:	APPLICATION:
Tuesday. Matthew 26:47–68	Psalm 55:12–14, 20–21
MEDITATION:	APPLICATION:

Wednesday. Matthew 26:69–27:20
MEDITATION: _____

Daniel 2:26–28; 4:24–27
APPLICATION: _____

_____

_____

_____

_____

Thursday. Matthew 27:21–44
MEDITATION: _____

Psalm 22:6–8; 42:1–4; 44:13–16
APPLICATION: _____

_____

_____

_____

_____

Friday. Matthew 27:45–28:10
MEDITATION: _____

Psalm 68:16–20; 16:8–10
APPLICATION: _____

_____

_____

_____

_____

Weekend. Matthew 28:11
MEDITATION: _____

1 Chronicles 16:23–25
APPLICATION: _____

_____

_____

_____

_____

MEMORY VERSE: Go therefore and make disciples of all the nations, baptizing them in the name of the Father and of the Son and of the Holy Spirit.

Matthew 28:19

~· Devotional ·~

MARK'S GOSPEL LAUNCHES US almost immediately into Jesus' Galilean ministry. He taught (Mark 1:1ff) and healed (1:27) with the authority of God Himself. He was criticized for declaring sins forgiven (2:7), for eating with sinners (2:16), and for healing on the Sabbath (3:2). He taught in parables (4:11), but explained everything to His disciples (4:34). He calmed the elements (4:41) and cast out demons (5:8). In every case, He demonstrated compassion, as in the healing of the woman with the issue of blood (5:26–34). Oh, how He loves you and me!

NEW TESTAMENT	OLD TESTAMENT
Monday. Mark 1:1–45	Psalm 31:14–16; 145:8–9
MEDITATION: _____	APPLICATION: _____
_____	_____
_____	_____
_____	_____
_____	_____
Tuesday. Mark 2:1–22	Isaiah 43:22–25; 53:10–12
MEDITATION: _____	APPLICATION: _____
_____	_____
_____	_____
_____	_____
_____	_____

Wednesday. Mark 2:23–3:27

MEDITATION: _____

_____

_____

_____

_____

1 Samuel 21:1–5; Isaiah 56:2

APPLICATION: _____

_____

_____

_____

_____

Thursday. Mark 3:28–4:20

MEDITATION: _____

_____

_____

_____

_____

Exodus 19:3–5

APPLICATION: _____

_____

_____

_____

_____

Friday. Mark 4:21–5:10

MEDITATION: _____

_____

_____

_____

_____

Psalm 29:3–5, 7, 10; 77:11–19

APPLICATION: _____

_____

_____

_____

_____

Weekend. Mark 5:11–36

MEDITATION: _____

_____

_____

_____

_____

1 Samuel 17:42–47, 50

APPLICATION: _____

_____

_____

_____

_____

MEMORY VERSE: When Jesus heard it, He said to them, "Those who are well have no need of a physician, but those who are sick. I did not come to call the righteous, but sinners, to repentance."

Mark 2:17

·- DEVOTIONAL ·-

PEOPLE WERE CONSTANTLY, AND MISTAKENLY, judging Jesus by
externals. The people of Nazareth did so because of familiarity (Mark 6:4ff).
The 5,000 did so because they were fed (6:41). The scribes and Pharisees
did so on the basis of their traditions (7:8–9). Jesus said our problems are
internal, of the heart. The disciples' hearts were hardened on occasion
(6:52). The leaders' hearts were far from God (7:6). It is what comes out of
the heart that defiles us (7:20–23), including our valuing people's opinions
more than God's (8:36–38). Where are our hearts fixed?

NEW TESTAMENT	OLD TESTAMENT
Monday. Mark 5:37–6:20	Deuteronomy 1:26–36
MEDITATION: _____	APPLICATION: _____
_____	_____
_____	_____
_____	_____
_____	_____
Tuesday. Mark 6:21–44	Psalm 145:1–7, 13–17; 69:30–34
MEDITATION: _____	APPLICATION: _____
_____	_____
_____	_____
_____	_____
_____	_____

Wednesday. Mark 6:45–7:13
MEDITATION: _____

_____
_____
_____
_____

Psalm 78:10–16, 32–39
APPLICATION: _____

_____
_____
_____
_____

Thursday. Mark 7:14–37
MEDITATION: _____

_____
_____
_____
_____

Proverbs: 6:12–19; Isaiah 59:2–3
APPLICATION: _____

_____
_____
_____
_____

Friday. Mark 8:1–26
MEDITATION: _____

_____
_____
_____
_____

Psalm 78:40–55
APPLICATION: _____

_____
_____
_____
_____

Weekend. Mark 8:27–9:13
MEDITATION: _____

_____
_____
_____
_____

Ecclesiastes 2:10–11; 12:13–14
APPLICATION: _____

_____
_____
_____
_____

MEMORY VERSE: For what will it profit a man if he gains the whole world, and loses his own soul?

Mark 8:36

∽· DEVOTIONAL ·∽

THE HARDEST LESSON WE HAVE TO LEARN is to trust God. The father of the demon-possessed young man had to cry for Jesus to help his unbelief (Mark 9:24ff). It takes the implicit faith of a child to be saved (10:15). The human tendency is to trust in ourselves, in our own means (10:24)—it takes God's grace to trust God instead (10:27), to see ourselves as servants and not masters (10:45). A servant of God who prays and trusts God to answer is the one who receives God's blessing (11:23). Jesus' enemies trusted in their own traditions, but erred out of ignorance of the Scriptures (12:24). In what, or whom, do we trust?

NEW TESTAMENT	OLD TESTAMENT
Monday. Mark 9:14–37	Exodus 33:7–11; Job 33:31–33
MEDITATION: _____	APPLICATION: _____
_____	_____
_____	_____
_____	_____
Tuesday. Mark 9:38–10:16	Genesis 39:6–12
MEDITATION: _____	APPLICATION: _____
_____	_____
_____	_____
_____	_____

Wednesday. Mark 10:17–41
MEDITATION: _____

_____
_____
_____
_____

Psalm 58:11; 73:24–26
APPLICATION: _____

_____
_____
_____
_____

Thursday. Mark 10:42–11:14
MEDITATION: _____

_____
_____
_____
_____

Genesis 22:1–2, 10–12; 24:35
APPLICATION: _____

_____
_____
_____
_____

Friday. Mark 11:15–12:12
MEDITATION: _____

_____
_____
_____
_____

Joshua 10:12–14; Psalm 145:18–19
APPLICATION: _____

_____
_____
_____
_____

Weekend. Mark 12:13–31
MEDITATION: _____

_____
_____
_____
_____

Proverbs 28:10; Psalm 140:1–8
APPLICATION: _____

_____
_____
_____
_____

MEMORY VERSE: Assuredly, I say to you, whoever does not receive the kingdom of God as a little child will by no means enter it.

Mark 10:15

⁓ DEVOTIONAL ⁓

AS THE END APPROACHED, Jesus tried to prepare His disciples by warning them that they too would face trials before rulers (Mark 13:9ff). Projecting ahead to the end of the age, He prophesied the destruction of the present physical universe but assured them His word would never pass away (13:31). After the Last Supper (14:24), Jesus went to Gethsemane to pray, again warning His disciples to watch and pray because the flesh is weak (14:38), as Peter later discovered (14:72). The mistreatment Jesus prophesied in His own case came true (15:16–20). God's Word is true.

NEW TESTAMENT	OLD TESTAMENT
Monday. Mark 12:32–13:10	Malachi 3:8–12; Exodus 35:4–9
MEDITATION:	APPLICATION:
Tuesday. Mark 13:11–37	Daniel 11:33–35; 9:26–27; Psalm 11
MEDITATION:	APPLICATION:

Wednesday. Mark 14:1–26   Exodus 12:1–12
MEDITATION: _____   APPLICATION: _____
_____   _____
_____   _____
_____   _____
_____   _____

Thursday. Mark 14:27–52   1 Kings 8:54–59; Daniel 6:10
MEDITATION: _____   APPLICATION: _____
_____   _____
_____   _____
_____   _____
_____   _____

Friday. Mark 14:53–15:5   Psalm 27:1–4; 26:1–6
MEDITATION: _____   APPLICATION: _____
_____   _____
_____   _____
_____   _____
_____   _____

Weekend. Mark 15:6–32   Psalm 22:16–31
MEDITATION: _____   APPLICATION: _____
_____   _____
_____   _____
_____   _____
_____   _____

MEMORY VERSE: Heaven and earth will pass away, but My words will by no means pass away.

Mark 13:31

~· DEVOTIONAL ·~

WHETHER ONE LOOKS AT THE CROSS (Mark 15:39f) and resurrection (16:9) at the end of the Lord's life or at the angel's announcement of the Virgin Birth to Mary (Luke 1:35ff) at the beginning of Jesus' life; whether one listens to Zachariah's prophecy about a visitation from on high (1:78) or the angel's announcement to the shepherds of the birth of the Savior (2:11), one thing is perfectly clear: Jesus Christ is the eternal Son of God and our Savior! He was certainly conscious of who He was, even as a boy (2:49). Are we conscious of God's will in our lives?

NEW TESTAMENT	OLD TESTAMENT
Monday. Mark 15:33–16:8	Psalm 69:19–21; Isaiah 35:3–10
MEDITATION: _____	APPLICATION: _____
_____	_____
_____	_____
_____	_____
_____	_____
Tuesday. Mark 16:9–Luke 1:13	Numbers 14:1–11
MEDITATION: _____	APPLICATION: _____
_____	_____
_____	_____
_____	_____
_____	_____

Wednesday. Luke 1:14–45

MEDITATION: _____

Judges 13:2–5, 24; Malachi 4:5–6

APPLICATION: _____

_____
_____
_____
_____

_____
_____
_____
_____

Thursday. Luke 1:46–79

MEDITATION: _____

Micah 7:18–20

APPLICATION: _____

_____
_____
_____
_____

_____
_____
_____
_____

Friday. Luke 1:80–2:26

MEDITATION: _____

Isaiah 12:2–5; Psalm 146:1–9

APPLICATION: _____

_____
_____
_____
_____

_____
_____
_____
_____

Weekend. Luke 2:27–52

MEDITATION: _____

1 Samuel 1:24–28; 3:4–10, 19–21

APPLICATION: _____

_____
_____
_____
_____

_____
_____
_____
_____

MEMORY VERSE: And the angel answered and said to her, "The Holy Spirit will come upon you, and the power of the Highest will overshadow you; therefore, also, that Holy One who is to be born will be called the Son of God."

Luke 1:35

~· DEVOTIONAL ·~

AMONG THE UNIQUE DETAILS Luke gives us, following his account of Jesus' baptism and the witness of His cousin, John the Baptist (Luke 3:16ff), are Jesus' lineage on Mary's side (3:23) and Jesus' announcement of His public ministry in Nazareth (4:18). Jesus' ministry included healing, casting out demons (who acknowledged Him as Christ, 4:41), and calling sinners to repentance (5:32). He declared Himself Lord of the Sabbath (6:5) and healed on the Sabbath (6:10), enraging the Jewish leaders. He spent much time in prayer, and invested Himself in the twelve He had chosen (6:12–13). In whom are we investing?

NEW TESTAMENT	OLD TESTAMENT
Monday. Luke 3:1–22	Isaiah 40:1–10
MEDITATION:	APPLICATION:
Tuesday. Luke 3:23–38	Isaiah 11:1–5; Jeremiah 33:14–18
MEDITATION:	APPLICATION:

Wednesday. Luke 4:1–31
MEDITATION: _____

Isaiah 61:1–3
APPLICATION: _____

Thursday. Luke 4:32–5:11
MEDITATION: _____

2 Kings 5:1, 5–10, 13–14
APPLICATION: _____

Friday. Luke 5:12–35
MEDITATION: _____

Psalm 5:3–10; 119:145–151
APPLICATION: _____

Weekend. Luke 5:36–6:23
MEDITATION: _____

Psalm 37:7–13; 17:6–9
APPLICATION: _____

MEMORY VERSE: Heaven and earth will pass away, but My words will by no means pass away.

Luke 21:33

⌣· DEVOTIONAL ·⌣

OBEDIENCE TO CHRIST'S COMMANDMENTS is the highest priority for the Christian. Whether it is His commandment to show mercy to our enemies (Luke 6:36ff), or His teaching of the need to build our lives on the rock of His commandments, or His parable about the seed that fell on good ground being obedient to the Word of God (8:15), it is clear that being an obedient child of God is greater than being the greatest prophet (7:28). If only we could be as obedient to Christ as the elements are (8:25)! Obedience includes serving Christ. Jesus sent out the twelve to preach the gospel and to heal the sick in His name and in His power (9:1–2). Upon their return, He took them apart for retreat (9:10). He refreshes those who serve Him.

NEW TESTAMENT	OLD TESTAMENT
Monday. Luke 6:24–45	1 Samuel 24:7–13, 16–21
MEDITATION:	APPLICATION:
Tuesday. Luke 6:46–7:23	Psalm 18:1–5, 16–24
MEDITATION:	APPLICATION:

Wednesday. Luke 7:24–50
MEDITATION: _____

_____
_____
_____
_____

Proverbs 26:12; Isaiah 5:20–22
APPLICATION: _____

_____
_____
_____
_____

Thursday. Luke 8:1–21
MEDITATION: _____

_____
_____
_____
_____

Psalm 78:1–4; Jeremiah 6:9–10
APPLICATION: _____

_____
_____
_____
_____

Friday. Luke 8:22–48
MEDITATION: _____

_____
_____
_____
_____

Psalm 33:18–22; 9:9–11
APPLICATION: _____

_____
_____
_____
_____

Weekend. Luke 8:49–9:17
MEDITATION: _____

_____
_____
_____
_____

2 Kings 4:42–44; Psalm 90:1–6
APPLICATION: _____

_____
_____
_____
_____

MEMORY VERSE: But why do you call me "Lord, Lord," and do not do the things which I say?

Luke 6:46

⌁· DEVOTIONAL ·⌁

WHAT WE THINK OF CHRIST determines our destiny. Jesus warned against being ashamed of Him (Luke 9:26ff) or turning back on our commitment to Him (9:62). Jesus is the only way to the Father (10:22); prayer to the Father must be persistent (11:9) and in Jesus' name. No wonder Jesus reacted strongly when some people attributed His miracles to the power of Satan (11:18) instead of God (11:20). For the same reason, Jesus warned against trying to please people instead of God, since God holds the keys to heaven and hell (12:5). Are we trying to please Christ?

NEW TESTAMENT

Monday. Luke 9:18–43
MEDITATION: _____
_____
_____
_____
_____

Tuesday. Luke 9:43–10:7
MEDITATION: _____
_____
_____
_____
_____

OLD TESTAMENT

Nehemiah 9:25–31
APPLICATION: _____
_____
_____
_____
_____

2 Samuel 22:22–30
APPLICATION: _____
_____
_____
_____
_____

Wednesday. Luke 10:8–29

MEDITATION: _____

_____

_____

_____

_____

Daniel 5:10–14; 1 Kings 4:29–34

APPLICATION: _____

_____

_____

_____

_____

Thursday. Luke 10:30–11:13

MEDITATION: _____

_____

_____

_____

_____

Proverbs 3:1–4, 27–28

APPLICATION: _____

_____

_____

_____

_____

Friday. Luke 11:14–36

MEDITATION: _____

_____

_____

_____

_____

Proverbs 4:18–27; Psalm 18:28

APPLICATION: _____

_____

_____

_____

_____

Weekend. Luke 11:37–12:7

MEDITATION: _____

_____

_____

_____

_____

Isaiah 51:7–8, 12–16; Psalm 56:3–4

APPLICATION: _____

_____

_____

_____

_____

MEMORY VERSE: So I say to you, ask, and it will be given to you; seek, and you will find; knock, and it will be opened to you.

Luke 11:9

↤· DEVOTIONAL ·↦

IT TAKES HUMILITY TO COME TO CHRIST and it takes humility to follow Christ. Failure to humble oneself and repent is to blaspheme against the Holy Spirit (Luke 12:10ff) and to perish forever (13:4). If we will but humble ourselves, Christ will lift us up (14:11). In the same way, if we would follow Christ as Lord we must be willing to sacrifice our own desires. Otherwise, we cannot be His disciples (14:33). The story of the prodigal [wasteful] son illustrates the need to humble ourselves and admit our spiritual bankruptcy. As soon as we take a step toward our heavenly Father, He throws His loving arms around us (15:20). Have we humbled ourselves before Him?

NEW TESTAMENT	OLD TESTAMENT
Monday. Luke 12:8–34	Proverbs 30:7–9; 23:4–5
MEDITATION: _____	APPLICATION: _____
_____	_____
_____	_____
_____	_____
Tuesday. Luke 12:35–56	Psalm 24:1–6; Isaiah 26:7–12
MEDITATION: _____	APPLICATION: _____
_____	_____
_____	_____
_____	_____

Wednesday: Luke 12:57–13:21
MEDITATION: _____

Isaiah 5:1–7, 15–16
APPLICATION: _____

_____
_____
_____
_____

Thursday. Luke 13:22–14:14
MEDITATION: _____

Isaiah 2:12–17; Proverbs 15:33
APPLICATION: _____

_____
_____
_____
_____

Friday. Luke 14:15–15:10
MEDITATION: _____

Daniel 3:16–20, 26–27
APPLICATION: _____

_____
_____
_____
_____

Weekend. Luke 15:11–16:8
MEDITATION: _____

Ezekiel 33:10–15; Jeremiah 18:7–8
APPLICATION: _____

_____
_____
_____
_____

MEMORY VERSE: Therefore you also be ready, for the Son of Man is coming at an hour you do not expect.

Luke 12:40

⌁· DEVOTIONAL ·⌁

JESUS PROPHESIED HIS SECOND COMING in such a way that vain speculation was precluded. The clear impression from a number of illustrations is that Jesus' return will be sudden, like a flash of lightning (Luke 17:24ff). Until then, we are to evangelize the lost for that is why Jesus came into the world the first time (19:10). Our faithfulness in using the opportunities He gives us will be the basis of reward when He returns (19:6). The hardhearted Jewish leaders were blinded to Jesus' purposes, and to His love (19:41). Are we?

NEW TESTAMENT	OLD TESTAMENT
Monday. Luke 16:9–17:4	Psalm 139:1–10, 13–14, 23–24
MEDITATION:	APPLICATION:
Tuesday. Luke 17:5–37	Genesis 19:1, 12–16
MEDITATION:	APPLICATION:

Wednesday. Luke 18:1–25

MEDITATION: _____

_____

_____

_____

_____

Jeremiah 9:23–24; Psalm 49:1–13

APPLICATION: _____

_____

_____

_____

_____

Thursday. Luke 18:26–19:10

MEDITATION: _____

_____

_____

_____

_____

Jonah 3:1–10; 2 Chronicles 31:1

APPLICATION: _____

_____

_____

_____

_____

Friday. Luke 19:11–40

MEDITATION: _____

_____

_____

_____

_____

Proverbs 12:14; 24:12

APPLICATION: _____

_____

_____

_____

_____

Weekend. Luke 19:41–20:19

MEDITATION: _____

_____

_____

_____

_____

Isaiah 1:10–17

APPLICATION: _____

_____

_____

_____

_____

MEMORY VERSE: No servant can serve two masters; for either he will hate the one and love the other, or else he will be loyal to the one and despise the other. You cannot serve God and mammon.

Luke 16:13

⌁ DEVOTIONAL ⌁

THE GOVERNMENTS OF THIS WORLD are used by Satan to oppose Christ. The Jewish leaders tried to use paying taxes as an issue against Jesus (Luke 20:25ff; 23:2). The Lord warned His disciples they would be persecuted before rulers (21:12). But God is in control; Jesus' words will not pass away (21:33). When and if we face official persecution, we must remember Jesus' willingness to die for us (22:42), His readiness to acknowledge who He was for our sake (22:70), and His promise to fill our mouth in the day of trial (21:14–15). Beyond this, we should be ready to forgive those who persecute us, as He did (23:34).

NEW TESTAMENT	OLD TESTAMENT
Monday. Luke 20:20–47	Micah 2:1–3; Ezekiel 34:1–4, 7–10
MEDITATION:	APPLICATION:
Tuesday. Luke 21:1–28	Exodus 4:10–11, 14–16
MEDITATION:	APPLICATION:

Wednesday. Luke 21:29–22:20

MEDITATION: _____

_____

_____

_____

_____

Psalm 119:57–60; 119:1–8

APPLICATION: _____

_____

_____

_____

_____

Thursday. Luke 22:21–53

MEDITATION: _____

_____

_____

_____

_____

Psalm 86:1–11; 143:9–10

APPLICATION: _____

_____

_____

_____

_____

Friday. Luke 22:54–23:12

MEDITATION: _____

_____

_____

_____

_____

Genesis 27:30–37, 41

APPLICATION: _____

_____

_____

_____

_____

Weekend. Luke 23:13–43

MEDITATION: _____

_____

_____

_____

_____

Isaiah 30:8–15,18; Jeremiah 36:2–3

APPLICATION: _____

_____

_____

_____

_____

MEMORY VERSES: And He was withdrawn from them about a stone's throw, and He knelt down and prayed, saying, "Father, if it is Your will, take this cup away from Me; nevertheless not My will, but Yours, be done."

Luke 22:41–42

~· DEVOTIONAL ·~

BOTH THE END OF LUKE and the beginning of John deal with the resurrection, the central historical fact of the Christian faith. The angels reminded the women on Easter morning that Jesus had predicted His resurrection in Galilee (Luke 24:6f). Jesus showed the two men on the road to Emmaus the Bible prophecies concerning Himself (24:32). It is faith in Christ (John 1:12f), the crucified "Lamb of God" (1:29), the One who predicted His own resurrection on His first visit to the temple (2:19), that saves. The one who believes in his heart that Christ has been raised from the dead is "born again" (3:3) and has eternal life (3:16). Have we received Christ by faith and been born of the Spirit?

NEW TESTAMENT	OLD TESTAMENT
Monday. Luke 23:44–24:12	Isaiah 42:1–9; 41:13–14
MEDITATION:	APPLICATION:
Tuesday. Luke 24:13–53	Deuteronomy 32:1–4; Isaiah 40:9
MEDITATION:	APPLICATION:

Wednesday. John 1:1–28
MEDITATION: _____

Psalm 118:22–29; Isaiah 9:2, 6
APPLICATION: _____

Thursday. John 1:29–51
MEDITATION: _____

Isaiah 53:4–12
APPLICATION: _____

Friday. John 2:1–25
MEDITATION: _____

Psalm 26:1–12; 69:6–9; 101:6–8
APPLICATION: _____

Weekend. John 3:1–30
MEDITATION: _____

Isaiah 59:12–17; 49:6
APPLICATION: _____

MEMORY VERSE: Jesus answered and said to him, "Most assuredly, I say to you, unless one is born again, he cannot see the kingdom of God."

John 3:3

~· DEVOTIONAL ·~

WHEREVER JESUS WENT, He met spiritual hunger that only He could satisfy. He helped the Samaritan woman to understand spiritual worship (John 4:23ff); He showed His disciples the Samaritans as a field ripe for harvest (4:35). He met physical needs through healing, earning Him opposition (5:18). He multiplied the loaves and fish to feed a hungry crowd (6:11), but made it clear that only faith in Him satisfies the soul (6:35). We should understand that people will not feel their need of Christ or come to Him until the Father sovereignly takes the initiative to draw them to Himself (6:44, 65). Are we praying for the Holy Spirit to open the blind eyes of the lost and convict them of their need of Christ (6:63, 68–69)?

NEW TESTAMENT	OLD TESTAMENT
Monday. John 3:31–4:26	Isaiah 12:1–6; Jeremiah 2:12–13
MEDITATION: _____	APPLICATION: _____
_____	_____
_____	_____
_____	_____
Tuesday. John 4:27–54	2 Chronicles 20:12–17, 20–24
MEDITATION: _____	APPLICATION: _____
_____	_____
_____	_____
_____	_____

Wednesday. John 5:1–29

MEDITATION: _____

_____

_____

_____

_____

Psalm 36:1–9; 34:21–22; 27:1

APPLICATION: _____

_____

_____

_____

_____

Thursday. John 5:30–6:15

MEDITATION: _____

_____

_____

_____

_____

Deuteronomy 18:15–22

APPLICATION: _____

_____

_____

_____

_____

Friday. John 6:16–40

MEDITATION: _____

_____

_____

_____

_____

Psalm 66:1–7; 114:1–8

APPLICATION: _____

_____

_____

_____

_____

Weekend. John 6:41–71

MEDITATION: _____

_____

_____

_____

_____

Numbers 13:17–21, 27–33

APPLICATION: _____

_____

_____

_____

_____

MEMORY VERSE: No one can come to Me unless the Father who sent Me draws him; and I will raise him up at the last day.

John 6:44

⌁ DEVOTIONAL ⌁

THE SECOND YEAR OF JESUS' public ministry was one filled with controversy. The people were divided in their opinion of Him (John 7:12ff). The leaders tried to trap Him, but Jesus caused the traps to backfire, as in the case of the woman caught in adultery (8:7). He made astounding claims to be equal with God (8:58), and once again healed someone on the Sabbath (9:14). The former blind man's simple testimony that once he was blind and now he saw (9:25) enraged the leaders (9:28, 34), as did Jesus' indictment that it was the leaders who were blind (9:41). In His dialogue with the leaders, Jesus said His only purpose as the "good shepherd" was to bring life more abundant to His sheep (10:10), to us!

NEW TESTAMENT	OLD TESTAMENT
Monday. John 7:1–31	Isaiah 66:2–5; 1 Kings 22:7–8
MEDITATION: _____	APPLICATION: _____
_____	_____
_____	_____
_____	_____
Tuesday. John 7:32–8:11	Psalm 14:1–3; Ecclesiastes 7:20
MEDITATION: _____	APPLICATION: _____
_____	_____
_____	_____
_____	_____

Wednesday. John 8:12–41
MEDITATION: _____

Psalm 2:2–12
APPLICATION: _____

_____

_____

_____

Thursday. John 8:42–9:12
MEDITATION: _____

Numbers 25:1–13
APPLICATION: _____

_____

_____

_____

Friday. John 9:13–41
MEDITATION: _____

Psalm 119:17–24; 146:5–10
APPLICATION: _____

_____

_____

_____

Weekend. John 10:1–33
MEDITATION: _____

Psalm 23:1–6; 100; Isaiah 40:11
APPLICATION: _____

_____

_____

_____

MEMORY VERSE: And you shall know the truth, and the truth shall make you free.

John 8:32

ᴅ ᴇᴠᴏᴛɪᴏɴᴀʟ ᴅ

THE EVENT THAT MOVED the Jewish leaders to act against Jesus was
His raising of Lazarus from the dead (John 11:43ff). This stunning
miracle so close to Jerusalem brought curiosity seekers to see Jesus and
Lazarus (12:9), and crowds to hail Jesus on Palm Sunday (12:13). Events
moved quickly after that, with Jesus warning those who did not believe of
judgment to come (12:48). Jesus' final days were filled with teaching His
disciples to serve (13:14) and to love one another (13:34), with words of
comfort that He would return for them (14:3), and with promises that He
would answer their prayers (14:14) and send the Holy Spirit to dwell within
them (14:17). In the meanwhile, they were (and we are) to obey Him
(14:23).

NEW TESTAMENT	OLD TESTAMENT
Monday. John 10:34–11:27	Psalm 40:1–5; Isaiah 25:1, 8–9
MEDITATION:	APPLICATION:
Tuesday. John 11:28–57	1 Kings 17:12–13, 15–17, 19–22, 24
MEDITATION:	APPLICATION:

Wednesday. John 12:1–26

MEDITATION: _____

_____

_____

_____

_____

Psalm 10:1–11, 14–16

APPLICATION: _____

_____

_____

_____

_____

Thursday. John 12:27–13:5

MEDITATION: _____

_____

_____

_____

_____

Numbers 11:10–15, 18, 21–23

APPLICATION: _____

_____

_____

_____

_____

Friday. John 13:6–35

MEDITATION: _____

_____

_____

_____

_____

Exodus 20:1–17

APPLICATION: _____

_____

_____

_____

_____

Weekend. John 13:36–14:26

MEDITATION: _____

_____

_____

_____

_____

Deuteronomy 11:1–10

APPLICATION: _____

_____

_____

_____

_____

MEMORY VERSES: A new commandment I give to you, that you love one another; as I have loved you, that you also love one another. By this all will know that you are My disciples, if you have love for one another.

John 13:34–35

~· DEVOTIONAL ·~

OUR PERSONAL RELATIONSHIP TO JESUS CHRIST entails total dependence on Him and on the truth of His Word (John 15:5ff). He promised that the Holy Spirit will guide us into all truth (16:13). It is through the truth of God's Word that we are sanctified (17:17) and that we come to believe on Christ in the first place (17:20). Christ came to bear witness to the truth and everyone who is of the truth, who is saved, believes the truth Christ reveals through His Word (18:37). When the Jewish leaders accused Jesus (correctly) of claiming to be the Son of God (19:7), this frightened Pilate (19:8) and he tried to release Jesus, finally caving in to the leaders' pressure (19:12). Out of spite, Pilate had a truthful sign nailed to the cross: "The King of the Jews" (19:19).

NEW TESTAMENT	OLD TESTAMENT
Monday. John 14:27–15:27	Psalm 51:10–13; 33:12–22
MEDITATION: _____	APPLICATION: _____
_____	_____
_____	_____
_____	_____
Tuesday. John 16:1–28	Isaiah 40:27–31; Psalm 37:3–6
MEDITATION: _____	APPLICATION: _____
_____	_____
_____	_____
_____	_____

Wednesday. John 16:29–17:19

MEDITATION: _____

_____

_____

_____

_____

Psalm 91:1–16

APPLICATION: _____

_____

_____

_____

_____

Thursday. John 17:20–18:18

MEDITATION: _____

_____

_____

_____

_____

Psalm 133:1–3; Isaiah 66:19–23

APPLICATION: _____

_____

_____

_____

_____

Friday. John 18:19–19:3

MEDITATION: _____

_____

_____

_____

_____

Psalm 117:1–2; 119:137–142

APPLICATION: _____

_____

_____

_____

_____

Weekend. John 19:4–27

MEDITATION: _____

_____

_____

_____

_____

2 Chronicles 20:5–6

APPLICATION: _____

_____

_____

_____

_____

MEMORY VERSE: I do not pray for these alone, but also for those who will believe in Me through their word.

John 17:20

‿· DEVOTIONAL ·‿

JESUS DIED OF A BROKEN HEART because of our sins, as became clear when blood and water issued from His side (John 19:34ff). He was buried (19:40–42); and He rose on the third day, appearing to ten of the apostles that evening and to Thomas eight days later (20:28). These facts do not exhaust the story of Jesus (21:25), but it was to these essential elements that they were to bear witness (Acts 1:8ff), which they did powerfully on Pentecost (2:4). The beginning of the church is a thrilling story: people gladly received the Word, were baptized, were instructed in doctrine, observed the Lord's Supper, met for fellowship and prayer (2:41–42), were filled with brotherly love (2:44–45) and joy (2:46), and had a wonderful testimony (2:47). Is this true of us?

NEW TESTAMENT	OLD TESTAMENT
Monday. John 19:28–20:9	Psalm 47:1–9; Isaiah 53:10–12
MEDITATION: _____	APPLICATION: _____
_____	_____
_____	_____
_____	_____
_____	_____
Tuesday: John 20:10–21:3	Judges 6:12–18, 36–37
MEDITATION: _____	APPLICATION: _____
_____	_____
_____	_____
_____	_____
_____	_____

Wednesday. John 21:4–25
MEDITATION: _____

Numbers 27:15–17; Ezekiel 34:1–6
APPLICATION: _____

_____
_____
_____
_____

Thursday. Acts 1:1–26
MEDITATION: _____

Psalm 98:1–6; 96:10–13
APPLICATION: _____

_____
_____
_____
_____

Friday. Acts 2:1–28
MEDITATION: _____

Isaiah 44:1–8
APPLICATION: _____

_____
_____
_____
_____

Weekend. Acts 2:29–3:10
MEDITATION: _____

Psalm 130:1–8; Hosea 6:1–3, 5–6
APPLICATION: _____

_____
_____
_____
_____

MEMORY VERSE: But you shall receive power when the Holy Spirit has come upon you; and you shall be witnesses to Me in Jerusalem, and in all Judea and Samaria, and to the end of the earth.

Acts 1:8

⌒· DEVOTIONAL ·⌒

THE HOLY SPIRIT TURNED PETER into a bold preacher who declared in his first encounter with the Jewish leaders that Jesus' name is the only one that saves (Acts 4:12ff). When Peter and John returned, the believers had a prayer and praise meeting that shook the place (4:31)! When the Sanhedrin arrested the apostles again, they said that they had to obey God and not man (5:29). After the deacons were ordained, God used Stephen in the same powerful way (6:10). During his trial, Stephen underscored the fact that the people of Israel rejected Moses' leadership on more than one occasion (7:27, 35, 39). He also pointed out Moses' prophecy of a Prophet to come whom the people would hear (7:37). The Holy Spirit can make us bold witnesses too!

NEW TESTAMENT	OLD TESTAMENT
Monday. Acts 3:11–4:12	Psalm 118:19–23; Isaiah 28:14–18
MEDITATION: _____	APPLICATION: _____
_____	_____
_____	_____
_____	_____
Tuesday. Acts 4:13–37	Isaiah 43:1–7, 11–13
MEDITATION: _____	APPLICATION: _____
_____	_____
_____	_____
_____	_____

Wednesday. Acts 5:1–26

MEDITATION: _____

Joshua 7:20–21, 24–25

APPLICATION: _____

Thursday. Acts 5:27–6:7

MEDITATION: _____

Isaiah 46:8–13; Ecclesiastes 3:14–15

APPLICATION: _____

Friday. Acts 6:8–7:16

MEDITATION: _____

Psalm 105:1–20

APPLICATION: _____

Weekend. Acts 7:17–42

MEDITATION: _____

Psalm 105:27–45

APPLICATION: _____

MEMORY VERSE: Nor is there salvation in any other, for there is no other name under heaven given among men by which we must be saved.

Acts 4:12

ᵔ· DEVOTIONAL ·ᵕ

AFTER THE SANHEDRIN STONED STEPHEN (Acts 7:59ff), another deacon, Philip, preached a revival in Samaria (8:5), leading Peter and John to go there. When Simon the sorcerer tried to buy the power to make the Holy Spirit fall, Peter rebuked him (8:20). Not long after, Saul of Tarsus was on his way to Damascus to persecute the church, when he met Jesus (9:5). After his conversion, Saul came to Jerusalem to join the disciples. He was befriended by Barnabas who introduced him to the apostles (9:27). Later, Peter had a vision in Joppa to prepare him for his first mission to the Gentiles (10:15). When he preached Jesus to the household of the Roman Centurion, Cornelius, and saw the Holy Spirit fall, it became clear to him that God had granted repentance to the Gentiles also (10:45). The gospel is for everyone!

NEW TESTAMENT	OLD TESTAMENT
Monday. Acts 7:42–8:1	2 Chronicles 24:18–22; 36:12–17
MEDITATION:	APPLICATION:
Tuesday. Acts 8:2–25	Numbers 16:1–3, 8–11, 28–35
MEDITATION:	APPLICATION:

Wednesday. Acts 8:26–9:9

MEDITATION: _____

_____

_____

_____

_____

Nehemiah 8:4–12

APPLICATION: _____

_____

_____

_____

_____

Thursday. Acts 9:10–35

MEDITATION: _____

_____

_____

_____

_____

1 Samuel 16:1–7, 11–12

APPLICATION: _____

_____

_____

_____

_____

Friday. Acts 9:36–10:23

MEDITATION: _____

_____

_____

_____

_____

Psalm 25:2–7; 1 Kings 9:1–3

APPLICATION: _____

_____

_____

_____

_____

Weekend. Acts 10:23–48

MEDITATION: _____

_____

_____

_____

_____

Isaiah 1:18–20; 55:7

APPLICATION: _____

_____

_____

_____

_____

MEMORY VERSE: And those of the circumcision who believed were astonished, as many as came with Peter, because the gift of the Holy Spirit had been poured out on the Gentiles also.

Acts 10:45

⌒· DEVOTIONAL ·⌒

JUST AS THE HOLY SPIRIT PROMPTED the local church at Antioch to commission Paul and Barnabas to go on the first missionary journey (Acts 13:2), so He is giving a new burst of missionary vision to local churches today, with many young people and adults answering the call to go on short-term mission trips. God's calling to help fulfill the Great Commission is not restricted to career missionaries, but is extended to each one of us. Are we listening?

NEW TESTAMENT	OLD TESTAMENT
Monday. Acts 11:1–30	Deuteronomy 15:4–10
MEDITATION: _____	APPLICATION: _____
_____	_____
_____	_____
_____	_____
Tuesday. Acts 12:1–25	Exodus 14:15–22, 31
MEDITATION: _____	APPLICATION: _____
_____	_____
_____	_____
_____	_____

Wednesday. Acts 13:1–25

MEDITATION: _____

_____
_____
_____
_____

Psalm 106:7–12; Exodus 4:31

APPLICATION: _____

_____
_____
_____
_____

Thursday. Acts 13:26–52

MEDITATION: _____

_____
_____
_____
_____

Psalm 92:1–8; 30:4–5, 11–12

APPLICATION: _____

_____
_____
_____
_____

Friday. Acts 14:1–28

MEDITATION: _____

_____
_____
_____
_____

1 Chronicles 14:9–14, 16–17

APPLICATION: _____

_____
_____
_____
_____

Weekend. Acts 15:1–21

MEDITATION: _____

_____
_____
_____
_____

Psalm 67:1–5; 22:27–28

APPLICATION: _____

_____
_____
_____
_____

MEMORY VERSE: But we believe that through the grace of the Lord Jesus Christ we shall be saved in the same manner as they.

Acts 15:11

~· Devotional ·~

THE APOSTLE PAUL WAS A PIONEER MISSIONARY at heart (see Romans 15:20–24). Because he was, Europe was opened up for the gospel. As a result of his second missionary journey, the gospel reached us some nineteen plus centuries later. With the knowledge that there are still thousands of people groups in the world today who do not have even one portion of Scripture in their own language, what should the emphasis of the church's missions programs be?

NEW TESTAMENT	OLD TESTAMENT
Monday. Acts 15:22–16:10	Proverbs 25:11; Ruth 2:8–12
MEDITATION: _____	APPLICATION: _____
_____	_____
_____	_____
_____	_____
Tuesday. Acts 16:11–34	Genesis 18:1–8; 2 Kings 4:8–1
MEDITATION: _____	APPLICATION: _____
_____	_____
_____	_____
_____	_____

Wednesday. Acts 16:35–17:15
MEDITATION: _____

_____
_____
_____
_____

Isaiah 55:10–11; Psalm 119:105
APPLICATION: _____

_____
_____
_____
_____

Thursday. Acts 17:16–18:4
MEDITATION: _____

_____
_____
_____
_____

Genesis 2:4–7; Job 38:1, 4–7, 22–25
APPLICATION: _____

_____
_____
_____
_____

Friday. Acts 18:5–28
MEDITATION: _____

_____
_____
_____
_____

Psalm 121:5–8; 46:1–3, 7
APPLICATION: _____

_____
_____
_____
_____

Weekend. Acts 19:1–22
MEDITATION: _____

_____
_____
_____
_____

2 Kings 11:17–18
APPLICATION: _____

_____
_____
_____
_____

MEMORY VERSE: For as I was passing through and considering the objects of your worship, I even found an altar with this inscription: TO THE UNKNOWN GOD. Therefore, the One whom you worship without knowing, Him I proclaim to you.

Acts 17:23

⌣· DEVOTIONAL ·⌣

PAUL'S DEVOTION TO THE LORD JESUS CHRIST and to the ministry of the gospel gave him a holy boldness, even as he returned to Jerusalem at the end of his third missionary journey with the knowledge that "chains and tribulations" awaited him (Acts 20:23). We do not know what price we may have to pay for standing up for our faith, but we do have the promise of the Lord Himself that He will never leave us nor forsake us (Matthew 28:20; Hebrews 13:5), a promise He kept to Paul (Acts 23:11).

NEW TESTAMENT	OLD TESTAMENT
Monday. Acts 19:23–20:6	Psalm 124:1–8; Nehemiah 4:7–9
MEDITATION:	APPLICATION:
Tuesday. Acts 20:7–38	1 Kings 19:4–10
MEDITATION:	APPLICATION:

Wednesday. Acts 21:1–25

MEDITATION: _____

_____

_____

_____

Exodus 32:1–4, 26–29

APPLICATION: _____

_____

_____

_____

Thursday. Acts 21:26–22:5

MEDITATION: _____

_____

_____

_____

Ezekiel 2:1–7; 3:4–11

APPLICATION: _____

_____

_____

_____

Friday. Acts 22:6–29

MEDITATION: _____

_____

_____

_____

Psalm 33:6–12; Jeremiah 29:11–13

APPLICATION: _____

_____

_____

_____

Weekend. Acts 22:30–23:22

MEDITATION: _____

_____

_____

_____

Psalm 75:1–10; 92:12–15

APPLICATION: _____

_____

_____

_____

MEMORY VERSE: But the following night the Lord stood by him and said, "Be of good cheer, Paul; for as you have testified for Me in Jerusalem so you must also bear witness at Rome."

Acts 23:11

⌐· DEVOTIONAL ·⌐

PAUL'S CHIEF DEFENSE AGAINST HIS ACCUSERS was the purity of
his life, his uprightness before the Law of God and the law of man (Acts
25:8ff; 26:4–5). This forced his enemies to trump up charges they could not
prove, and led the Roman governor and King Agrippa to conclude he had
done nothing worthy of death or imprisonment (26:31). Had he not
appealed to Caesar, he might have been set free (26:32). If we were charged
with being a Christian, would there be enough evidence to convict us?

NEW TESTAMENT	OLD TESTAMENT
Monday. Acts 23:23–24:16	2 Chronicles 31:20–21
MEDITATION:	APPLICATION:
Tuesday. Acts 24:17–25:12	Genesis 3:7–10; Nahum 1:2, 6
MEDITATION:	APPLICATION:

Wednesday. Acts 25:13–26:8

MEDITATION: _____

_____

_____

_____

2 Samuel 22:21–25; Psalm 37:17

APPLICATION: _____

_____

_____

_____

Thursday. Acts 26:9–32

MEDITATION: _____

_____

_____

_____

Exodus 15:11–14; 2 Samuel 7:18

APPLICATION: _____

_____

_____

_____

Friday. Acts 27:1–26

MEDITATION: _____

_____

_____

_____

Joshua 1:1–9; 1 Kings 8:56

APPLICATION: _____

_____

_____

_____

Weekend. Acts 27:27–28:10

MEDITATION: _____

_____

_____

_____

Psalm 107:23–30; Jonah 1:4–5, 12

APPLICATION: _____

_____

_____

_____

MEMORY VERSE: Then Agrippa said to Paul, "You almost persuade me to become a Christian."

Acts 26:28

⁓ DEVOTIONAL ⁓

THE BANNER CRY OF THE REFORMATION was "justification by faith." Paul was writing in Romans to both Jewish and Gentile Christians to clarify the basis of their salvation. The righteousness we need to enter heaven is not our own, but Christ's. We have His perfect character and merit credited to us by faith, by believing in and receiving the benefit of His atoning death on the cross and His resurrection from the dead. All of this is ours when we receive Jesus Christ as Savior and Lord.

NEW TESTAMENT	OLD TESTAMENT
Monday. Acts 28:11–31	Genesis 24:17–33
MEDITATION: _____	APPLICATION: _____
_____	_____
_____	_____
_____	_____
Tuesday. Romans 1:1–27	Psalm 19:1–4; 119:89–91; 97:1–6
MEDITATION: _____	APPLICATION: _____
_____	_____
_____	_____
_____	_____

Wednesday. Romans 1:28–2:16

MEDITATION: _____

_____

_____

_____

_____

Psalm 94:1–15; Proverbs 5:21–23

APPLICATION: _____

_____

_____

_____

_____

Thursday. Romans 2:17–3:18

MEDITATION: _____

_____

_____

_____

_____

Jeremiah 7:3, 5–7; Micah 3:8–12

APPLICATION: _____

_____

_____

_____

_____

Friday. Romans 3:19–4:12

MEDITATION: _____

_____

_____

_____

_____

Genesis 15:1–6; Psalm 20:6–8

APPLICATION: _____

_____

_____

_____

_____

Weekend. Romans 4:13–5:11

MEDITATION: _____

_____

_____

_____

_____

Psalm 69:13; 62:5–6; Isaiah 63:7–9

APPLICATION: _____

_____

_____

_____

_____

MEMORY VERSES: For I am not ashamed of the gospel of Christ, for it is the power of God to salvation for everyone who believes, for the Jew first and also for the Greek. For in it the righteousness of God is revealed from faith to faith; as it is written, "The just shall live by faith."

Romans 1:16–17

⌣· DEVOTIONAL ·⌣

ONCE WE RECEIVE CHRIST'S RIGHTEOUSNESS—His life; by faith, we have eternal life. But this eternal life is not just an eternal extension of this life; it is a brand new life, and a new lifestyle. We have Christ living in us when the Holy Spirit enters our hearts upon receiving Christ by faith as Savior and Lord (Romans 8:9f). The presence of the Holy Spirit gives us new life in Christ, and a new power for living in accordance with God's righteous commandments (8:4).

NEW TESTAMENT	OLD TESTAMENT
Monday. Romans 5:12–6:14	Isaiah 1:4; Jeremiah 3:19–23
MEDITATION: _____	APPLICATION: _____
_____	_____
_____	_____
_____	_____
Tuesday. Romans 6:15–7:13	Psalm 95:6–7; Deuteronomy 7:6–8
MEDITATION: _____	APPLICATION: _____
_____	_____
_____	_____
_____	_____

Wednesday. Romans 7:14–8:17

MEDITATION: _____

_____

_____

_____

_____

Joshua 24:1, 14–18, 25–26

APPLICATION: _____

_____

_____

_____

_____

Thursday. Romans 8:18–39

MEDITATION: _____

_____

_____

_____

_____

Isaiah 59:12–17, 21

APPLICATION: _____

_____

_____

_____

_____

Friday. Romans 9:1–29

MEDITATION: _____

_____

_____

_____

_____

Isaiah 45:6–7, 9; Job 40:1–8

APPLICATION: _____

_____

_____

_____

_____

Weekend. Romans 9:30–10:21

MEDITATION: _____

_____

_____

_____

_____

Leviticus 18:1–5; Psalm 19:1–4

APPLICATION: _____

_____

_____

_____

_____

MEMORY VERSE: There is therefore now no condemnation to those who are in Christ Jesus, who do not walk according to the flesh, but according to the Spirit.

Romans 8:1

⌒· DEVOTIONAL ·⌒

IN READING ALL OF PAUL'S LETTERS, it is clear that he bases his admonitions for Christian living on the truth of Christian doctrine. Conversely, doctrinal truth always has practical implications. Those who are forgiven based on faith in the work of Christ need to forgive others (see Romans 14:10). If Christ loved us, we need to love one another (see Romans 13:8–10). Being a child of God impacts absolutely every relationship we have.

NEW TESTAMENT	OLD TESTAMENT
Monday. Romans 11:1–21	Ezekiel 18:21–23; Psalm 85:7–13
MEDITATION: _____	APPLICATION: _____
_____	_____
_____	_____
_____	_____
Tuesday. Romans 11:22–12:8	1 Samuel 15:13–23
MEDITATION: _____	APPLICATION: _____
_____	_____
_____	_____
_____	_____

Wednesday. Romans 12:9–13:14

MEDITATION: _____

_____

_____

_____

Psalm 37:21, 26; 112:4–9

APPLICATION: _____

_____

_____

_____

Thursday. Romans 14:1–15:3

MEDITATION: _____

_____

_____

_____

Ecclesiastes 12:13–14

APPLICATION: _____

_____

_____

_____

Friday. Romans 15:4–29

MEDITATION: _____

_____

_____

_____

Psalm 33:18–22; 119:49–50

APPLICATION: _____

_____

_____

_____

Weekend. Romans 15:30–16:27

MEDITATION: _____

_____

_____

_____

Deuteronomy 13:4–10

APPLICATION: _____

_____

_____

_____

MEMORY VERSES: I beseech you therefore, brethren, by the mercies of God, that you present your bodies a living sacrifice, holy, acceptable to God, which is your reasonable service. And do not be conformed to this world, but be transformed by the renewing of your mind, that you may prove what is that good and acceptable and perfect will of God.

Romans 12:1–2

⌐· DEVOTIONAL ·⌐

CORINTH HAD THE REPUTATION of being a fleshly city, and the church there imbibed the ways of the world. There was divisiveness, intellectual pride, and sexual immorality—all problems in the church today as much as then. Paul had to get down to the basics of the Christian life and the Christian message because of the immaturity of the Corinthians. He wanted to lead them into the deeper things of Christ, but first they had to master the basics. So must we.

NEW TESTAMENT	OLD TESTAMENT
Monday. 1 Corinthians 1:1–25	Job 12:12–13, 16–25
MEDITATION:	APPLICATION:
Tuesday. 1 Corinthians 1:26–2:16	Job 28:13–28
MEDITATION:	APPLICATION:

Wednesday. 1 Corinthians 3:1–4:5

MEDITATION: _____

_____

_____

_____

Psalm 118:22; Zechariah 13:8–9

APPLICATION: _____

_____

_____

_____

Thursday. 1 Corinthians 4:6–5:8

MEDITATION: _____

_____

_____

_____

Deuteronomy 17:2–7, 12–13

APPLICATION: _____

_____

_____

_____

Friday. 1 Corinthians 5:9–6:20

MEDITATION: _____

_____

_____

_____

Numbers 25:1–3, 6–13

APPLICATION: _____

_____

_____

_____

Weekend. 1 Corinthians 7:1–24

MEDITATION: _____

_____

_____

_____

Proverbs 18:22; Malachi 2:13–16

APPLICATION: _____

_____

_____

_____

MEMORY VERSE: But the natural man does not receive the things of the Spirit of God, for they are foolishness to him; nor can he know them, because they are spiritually discerned.

1 Corinthians 2:14

⌁· DEVOTIONAL ·⌁

SOME OF THE BASICS PAUL DEALT WITH included marriage and divorce, Christian liberty and the body of Christ, authority in the church and home, gifts of the Spirit, and the love that Christ gives. In the end, if the Holy Spirit controls my life, I can deal with temptation and demonstrate the love of Christ toward others. If self is on the throne of my life, I will seek to gratify my own desires at the expense of others.

NEW TESTAMENT	OLD TESTAMENT
Monday. 1 Corinthians 7:25–8:8	Jeremiah 1:4–10; 16:1–2
MEDITATION: _____	APPLICATION: _____
_____	_____
_____	_____
_____	_____
_____	_____
Tuesday. 1 Corinthians 8:9–9:18	Amos 2:11–16; Numbers 6:1–8
MEDITATION: _____	APPLICATION: _____
_____	_____
_____	_____
_____	_____

Wednesday. 1 Corinthians 9:19
MEDITATION: _____

_____
_____
_____
_____

Genesis 3:1–6; Job 2:3, 6–7, 9–10
APPLICATION: _____

_____
_____
_____
_____

Thursday. 1 Corinthians 10:23
MEDITATION: _____

_____
_____
_____
_____

1 Samuel 2:12, 17, 22–25, 29–31
APPLICATION: _____

_____
_____
_____
_____

Friday. 1 Corinthians 11:23–12:13
MEDITATION: _____

_____
_____
_____
_____

Deuteronomy 34:9; Isaiah 11:1–2
APPLICATION: _____

_____
_____
_____
_____

Weekend. 1 Corinthians 12:14
MEDITATION: _____

_____
_____
_____
_____

Ruth 2:14–20
APPLICATION: _____

_____
_____
_____
_____

MEMORY VERSE: No temptation has overtaken you except such as is common to man; but God is faithful, who will not allow you to be tempted beyond what you are able, but with the temptation will also make the way of escape, that you may be able to bear it.

1 Corinthians 10:13

⌁ DEVOTIONAL ⌁

PAUL TAUGHT ORDERLINESS IN CHURCH WORSHIP and the exercise of spiritual gifts. He also made clear what is the heart of the gospel (1 Corinthians 15:3–4f), including Christ's resurrection. Paul underscores the serious consequences of denying the bodily resurrection of Jesus Christ, and then affirms His resurrection (and ours). He encourages us by telling us that our service for Christ is not in vain (15:58), and teaches us about systematic giving in the church. Paul had a pastor's heart and grounded the churches he established in solid Christian doctrine. Our pulpits and Sunday school classes must do the same.

NEW TESTAMENT	OLD TESTAMENT
Monday. 1 Corinthians 14:1–25	1 Kings 13:1–3; 2 Kings 23:13–16
MEDITATION:	APPLICATION:
Tuesday. 1 Corinthians 14:26–15:11	Isaiah 53:4–10; Psalm 47:5–8
MEDITATION:	APPLICATION:

Wednesday. 1 Corinthians 15:12–44   Isaiah 25:6–8; Daniel 12:1–3
MEDITATION: _____   APPLICATION: _____
_____   _____
_____   _____
_____   _____
_____   _____

Thursday. 1 Corinthians 15:44   Jeremiah 18:18; Psalm 35:1, 7–8
MEDITATION: _____   APPLICATION: _____
_____   _____
_____   _____
_____   _____
_____   _____

Friday. 2 Corinthians 1:1–17   Psalm 56:1–4; 119:64–80
MEDITATION: _____   APPLICATION: _____
_____   _____
_____   _____
_____   _____
_____   _____

Weekend. 2 Corinthians 1:18–3:3   Genesis 50:15–21; Psalm 32:1–6
MEDITATION: _____   APPLICATION: _____
_____   _____
_____   _____
_____   _____
_____   _____

MEMORY VERSE: Therefore, my beloved brethren, be steadfast, immovable, always abounding in the work of the Lord, knowing that your labor is not in vain in the Lord.

1 Corinthians 15:58

⌣· DEVOTIONAL ·⌣

THE GREATEST HARM TO THE WITNESS of the church of the Lord
Jesus Christ in our day has been the spectacle of professing Christian leaders
who have been led astray into impurity and thereby have given occasion to
the enemies of the gospel to ridicule the cause of Christ. Paul had to plead
with the Corinthians to maintain their purity in a dark and sinful world, to
separate themselves from the fleshly society in which they lived. So must we!

NEW TESTAMENT	OLD TESTAMENT
Monday. 2 Corinthians 3:4–4:15	Isaiah 5:11–12; Proverbs 4:18–19
MEDITATION:	APPLICATION:
Tuesday. 2 Corinthians 4:16–6:2	Psalm 24:3–10; Isaiah 60:1, 18–20
MEDITATION:	APPLICATION:

Wednesday. 2 Corinthians 6:3–7:7
MEDITATION: _____

Psalm 119:1–3, 9–11; 18:25–26
APPLICATION: _____

Thursday. 2 Corinthians 7:8–8:15
MEDITATION: _____

Ezra 10:1–5, 10–11, 14–16
APPLICATION: _____

Friday. 2 Corinthians 8:16–9:15
MEDITATION: _____

Deuteronomy 14:22–29
APPLICATION: _____

Weekend. 2 Corinthians 10:1–11:4
MEDITATION: _____

Jeremiah 23:25–29
APPLICATION: _____

MEMORY VERSE: Therefore, if anyone is in Christ, he is a new creation; old things have passed away; behold, all things have become new.

2 Corinthians 5:17

ᵕ· DEVOTIONAL ·ᵕ

GALATIANS IS NOTHING IF IT IS NOT A LETTER setting forth the grace of God as the basis of our salvation. The law convicts all of us as sinners and we stand condemned under the law. The glorious gospel of God's free gift of grace, His unmerited favor in granting us forgiveness for all of our sins based on faith in Christ's crucifixion and resurrection has set us free from our sentence of spiritual death and has given us eternal life!

NEW TESTAMENT	OLD TESTAMENT
Monday. 2 Corinthians 11:5–33	Exodus 1:11–14, 22; 2:1–3, 5, 7–10
MEDITATION:	APPLICATION:
Tuesday. 2 Corinthians 12:1–13:4	Exodus 14:13–14
MEDITATION:	APPLICATION:

Wednesday. 2 Corinthians 13:5   1 Chronicles 17:7–9, 11
MEDITATION: _____   APPLICATION: _____
_____   _____
_____   _____
_____   _____
_____   _____

Thursday. Galatians 1:21–2:21   Nehemiah 8:9–10
MEDITATION: _____   APPLICATION: _____
_____   _____
_____   _____
_____   _____
_____   _____

Friday. Galatians 3:1–20   Genesis 22:15–18; 1 Kings 2:1–4
MEDITATION: _____   APPLICATION: _____
_____   _____
_____   _____
_____   _____
_____   _____

Weekend. Galatians 3:21–4:20   Isaiah 64:8–9; Deuteronomy 14:2
MEDITATION: _____   APPLICATION: _____
_____   _____
_____   _____
_____   _____
_____   _____

MEMORY VERSE: I have been crucified with Christ; it is no longer I who
live, but Christ lives in me; and the life which I now live in the flesh I live
by faith in the Son of God, who loved me and gave Himself for me.

Galatians 2:20

ᴅᴇᴠᴏᴛɪᴏɴᴀʟ

PAUL PLEADED WITH THE EPHESIANS to strive to keep the unity produced by the Spirit (Ephesians 4:3f). We believers form the body of Christ (4:12), and we need each other—we need the gifts of grace God has distributed among us for the purpose of building up one another (4:16). No believer is an island; God has attached us to one another for the work of the ministry. Let us reach out to fellow believers with arms of love, just as He loves us.

NEW TESTAMENT	OLD TESTAMENT
Monday. Galatians 4:21–5:15	Genesis 15:1–4; 16:1–4; 21:8–12
MEDITATION: _____	APPLICATION: _____
_____	_____
_____	_____
_____	_____
Tuesday. Galatians 5:16–6:18	Ecclesiastes 2:26; Proverbs 3:3–4
MEDITATION: _____	APPLICATION: _____
_____	_____
_____	_____
_____	_____

Wednesday. Ephesians 1:1–2:3
MEDITATION: _____

Daniel 2:14–18; Job 42:7–9
APPLICATION: _____

_____

_____

_____

_____

_____

_____

Thursday. Ephesians 2:4–3:6
MEDITATION: _____

Isaiah 57:16–19; Micah 7:18–19
APPLICATION: _____

_____

_____

_____

_____

_____

_____

Friday. Ephesians 3:7–4:16
MEDITATION: _____

1 Chronicles 16:28–29, 34
APPLICATION: _____

_____

_____

_____

_____

_____

_____

Weekend. Ephesians 4:17–5:14
MEDITATION: _____

Proverbs 1:10, 15–19; 28:20
APPLICATION: _____

_____

_____

_____

_____

_____

_____

MEMORY VERSES: For by grace you have been saved through faith, and that not of yourselves; it is the gift of God, not of works, lest anyone should boast.

Ephesians 2:8–9

⌣· DEVOTIONAL ·⌣

IN PHILIPPIANS, PAUL EXHORTS THE CHURCH to have the attitude
of humility demonstrated by Christ (Philippians 2:5–8). Throughout the
letter, he exudes joy and encourages the Philippians to rejoice in the Lord
(1:25–26; 2:17–18; 3:1, 3; 4:4, 10). The secret to having the peace and joy
of the Lord is to bring everything to the Lord in prayer (4:6), to focus our
thinking exclusively on those things that flow from the mind and character
of God Himself (4:8), and to live and practice what God's Word teaches
(4:9).

NEW TESTAMENT	OLD TESTAMENT
Monday. Ephesians 5:15–6:4	Proverbs 5:18–20
MEDITATION: _____	APPLICATION: _____
_____	_____
_____	_____
_____	_____
Tuesday. Ephesians 6:5–24	Job 1:6–10; Daniel 10:4–7, 12–13
MEDITATION: _____	APPLICATION: _____
_____	_____
_____	_____
_____	_____

Wednesday. Philippians 1:1–2:4   Proverbs 22:4; 27:2
MEDITATION: _____   APPLICATION: _____

_____   _____

_____   _____

_____   _____

_____   _____

Thursday. Philippians 2:5–30   Psalm 34:12–14; 78:17–21
MEDITATION: _____   APPLICATION: _____

_____   _____

_____   _____

_____   _____

_____   _____

Friday. Philippians 3:1–21   Psalm 42:1–2; 63:1–8
MEDITATION: _____   APPLICATION: _____

_____   _____

_____   _____

_____   _____

_____   _____

Weekend. Philippians 4:1–23   Psalm 55:22; 105:1–4; 37:3–5
MEDITATION: _____   APPLICATION: _____

_____   _____

_____   _____

_____   _____

_____   _____

MEMORY VERSE: Finally, brethren, whatever things are true, whatever things are noble, whatever things are just, whatever things are pure, whatever things are lovely, whatever things are of good report, if there is any virtue and if there is anything praiseworthy—meditate on these things.

Philippians 4:8

~· DEVOTIONAL ·~

PAUL BATTLED AN EARLY HERESY in the Colossian church that has come back to haunt us in a new form as the New Age movement. Jewish Gnostics agreed with the Greek philosophy of their day, which put down the physical and glorified the spiritual, or immaterial. Specifically, these Gnostics claimed to have mystical experiences and contacts with a whole hierarchy of angelic beings descending from a pure spirit. Christ is above all created spirit beings; He is equal with God as the Creator (Colossians 1:16f) and has an exclusive position as our Savior. He left heaven to dwell in a body and, through the Spirit, in us (1:27)!

NEW TESTAMENT	OLD TESTAMENT
Monday. Colossians 1:1–23	Psalm 102:12, 15–22, 25–27
MEDITATION: _____	APPLICATION: _____
_____	_____
_____	_____
_____	_____
Tuesday. Colossians 1:24–2:15	Psalm 40:1–4; Proverbs 4:13–15
MEDITATION: _____	APPLICATION: _____
_____	_____
_____	_____
_____	_____

Wednesday. Colossians 2:16–3:17

MEDITATION: _____

_____

_____

_____

_____

Leviticus 19:1–4, 11–18, 37

APPLICATION: _____

_____

_____

_____

_____

Thursday. Colossians 3:18–4:18

MEDITATION: _____

_____

_____

_____

_____

Deuteronomy 21:18–21

APPLICATION: _____

_____

_____

_____

_____

Friday. 1 Thessalonians 1:1–2:16

MEDITATION: _____

_____

_____

_____

_____

Deuteronomy 7:6–8; Psalm 40:4–9

APPLICATION: _____

_____

_____

_____

_____

Weekend. 1 Thessalonians 2:17–4:12

MEDITATION: _____

_____

_____

_____

_____

Leviticus 22:31–33; 11:44–45

APPLICATION: _____

_____

_____

_____

_____

MEMORY VERSE: If then you were raised with Christ, seek those things which are above, where Christ is, sitting at the right hand of God.

Colossians 3:1

~· DEVOTIONAL ·~

IN BOTH 1 AND 2 THESSALONIANS, Paul clarifies issues surrounding the second coming of our Lord Jesus Christ in order to encourage and comfort the believers of Thessalonica (1 Thessalonians 4:18). They were not to be led astray by false prophecies of Christ's return (2 Thessalonians 2:2–3ff); not to stop working because of belief in His soon coming (3:11–12). Instead, they were to continue obeying the Word of God (2:15; 3:13), and to be found ready for Christ's return. Are you ready?

NEW TESTAMENT	OLD TESTAMENT
Monday. 1 Thessalonians 4:13–5:28	Job 19:25–27; Psalm 98:2–9
MEDITATION:	APPLICATION:
Tuesday. 2 Thessalonians 1:1–2:12	Isaiah 1:27–31; Proverbs 1:24–29
MEDITATION:	APPLICATION:

Wednesday. 2 Thessalonians 2:13
MEDITATION: _____

Proverbs 31:10–31; Ecclesiastes 2:26
APPLICATION: _____

_____
_____
_____
_____

Thursday. 1 Timothy 1:1–20
MEDITATION: _____

Jeremiah 33:6–9, 11; Isaiah 55:7
APPLICATION: _____

_____
_____
_____
_____

Friday. 1 Timothy 2:1–3:13
MEDITATION: _____

Deuteronomy 4:34–40
APPLICATION: _____

_____
_____
_____
_____

Weekend. 1 Timothy 3:14–4:16
MEDITATION: _____

2 Kings 22:1–2; 23:1–3, 24–25
APPLICATION: _____

_____
_____
_____
_____

MEMORY VERSES: For the Lord Himself will descend from heaven with a shout, with the voice of an archangel, and with the trumpet of God. And the dead in Christ will rise first. Then we who are alive and remain shall be caught up together with them in the clouds to meet the Lord in the air. And thus we shall always be with the Lord.

1 Thessalonians 4:16–17

⌣· DEVOTIONAL ·⌣

IN 1 TIMOTHY, PAUL EXHORTS his young protégé, Timothy, to be a
faithful minister, teaching the doctrine that Paul had taught him, avoiding
foolish, distracting questions (4:6–7). In 2 Timothy, Paul is facing execution
and writes to Timothy his last charge, expressing his own confidence in
God's faithfulness and power to keep him (1:12). He commends Timothy to
the inspired Scripture as the resource for every good work (3:14–17). Paul's
testimony was that he had fought a good fight, completed his work for
Christ, and kept the faith (4:7). May that be our life testimony as well!

NEW TESTAMENT	OLD TESTAMENT
Monday. 1 Timothy 5:1–25	2 Samuel 12:7–9, 13–14
MEDITATION: _____	APPLICATION: _____
_____	_____
_____	_____
_____	_____
Tuesday. 1 Timothy 6:1–21	Deuteronomy 8:11–14, 17–18
MEDITATION: _____	APPLICATION: _____
_____	_____
_____	_____
_____	_____

Wednesday. 2 Timothy 1:1–2:13

MEDITATION: _____

_____

_____

_____

_____

Deuteronomy 4:9–10; 31:9–13

APPLICATION: _____

_____

_____

_____

_____

Thursday. 2 Timothy 2:14–3:11

MEDITATION: _____

_____

_____

_____

_____

Proverbs 4:14–17, 20–27

APPLICATION: _____

_____

_____

_____

_____

Friday. 2 Timothy 3:12–4:22

MEDITATION: _____

_____

_____

_____

_____

Nehemiah 8:1–3, 8, 14–18

APPLICATION: _____

_____

_____

_____

_____

Weekend. Titus 1:1–2:8

MEDITATION: _____

_____

_____

_____

_____

Isaiah 50:4–7; Leviticus 22:9

APPLICATION: _____

_____

_____

_____

_____

MEMORY VERSE: For this reason I also suffer these things; nevertheless I am not ashamed, for I know whom I have believed and am persuaded that He is able to keep what I have committed to Him until that Day.

2 Timothy 1:12

⌒ DEVOTIONAL ⌒

JUST AS PAUL TAUGHT HIS SON in the faith, Timothy (see 1 Timothy 6:1–2), so he teaches another son in the faith, Titus (see Titus 2:9–10), that servants are to obey and honor their earthly masters. He went so far as to return a runaway slave, Onesimus (whom Paul led to Christ in Rome), to his believing master, Philemon. Paul did not make an issue of slavery, believing in the soon return of Christ (Titus 2:13). But he went a long way toward planting the seeds of Onesimus' emancipation when he urged Philemon (whom he had also led to Christ, see Philemon 19) to receive his former slave not as a servant but as a beloved brother (Philemon 16). The principles of faithful service that Paul teaches apply to employee-employer relations as part of a witness for Christ.

NEW TESTAMENT	OLD TESTAMENT
Monday. Titus 2:9–3:15	Daniel 6:11–16, 19–23, 25–27
MEDITATION: _____	APPLICATION: _____
_____	_____
_____	_____
_____	_____
Tuesday. Philemon 1–25	Genesis 37:18–20, 26–28; 41:39
MEDITATION: _____	APPLICATION: _____
_____	_____
_____	_____
_____	_____

Wednesday. Hebrews 1:1–2:4
MEDITATION: _____

Exodus 15:1–3, 6–7
APPLICATION: _____

_____

_____

_____

_____

_____

_____

_____

_____

Thursday. Hebrews 2:5–3:6
MEDITATION: _____

Ezekiel 37:22–28; Isaiah 43:1, 25–28
APPLICATION: _____

_____

_____

_____

_____

_____

_____

_____

_____

Friday. Hebrews 3:7–4:13
MEDITATION: _____

Numbers 14:2–3, 6–9, 20–23
APPLICATION: _____

_____

_____

_____

_____

_____

_____

_____

_____

Weekend. Hebrews 4:14–6:8
MEDITATION: _____

Genesis 14:18–20; Exodus 28:1–3
APPLICATION: _____

_____

_____

_____

_____

_____

_____

_____

_____

MEMORY VERSES: Not by works of righteousness which we have done, but according to His mercy He saved us, through the washing of regeneration and renewing of the Holy Spirit. . . . This is a faithful saying, and these things I want you to affirm constantly, that those who have believed in God should be careful to maintain good works. These things are good and profitable to man.

Titus 3:5, 8

~· Devotional ·~

DO WE CONSIDER THE ANGELS, or Moses, or the high priest under the Law? Christ is superior to each one (see Hebrews 1–5). Citing the Old Testament example of Melchizedek, the priest of Salem to whom Abraham paid tithes (making Melchizedek his superior), the writer of Hebrews says Christ our high priest is similarly superior, offering Himself once and for all as a sacrifice for our sins, establishing a new and superior covenant, and calling for us to commit ourselves to Him in faith and not draw back in unbelief (Hebrews 6–10).

NEW TESTAMENT	OLD TESTAMENT
Monday. Hebrews 6:9–7:10	Psalm 89:20, 26–37; Joshua 23:4–6
MEDITATION:	APPLICATION:
Tuesday. Hebrews 7:11–8:6	Psalm 110:1–4; Jeremiah 31:33
MEDITATION:	APPLICATION:

Wednesday. Hebrews 8:7–9:12

MEDITATION: _____

_____

_____

_____

_____

Psalm 103:8–12; 111:7–9

APPLICATION: _____

_____

_____

_____

_____

Thursday. Hebrews 9:13–10:10

MEDITATION: _____

_____

_____

_____

_____

Exodus 24:3–7; Leviticus 16:15–17

APPLICATION: _____

_____

_____

_____

_____

Friday. Hebrews 10:11–39

MEDITATION: _____

_____

_____

_____

_____

Isaiah 66:10, 14–16; Amos 5:4–5

APPLICATION: _____

_____

_____

_____

_____

Weekend. Hebrews 11:1–22

MEDITATION: _____

_____

_____

_____

_____

Genesis 15:5–6; 6:9, 11–22

APPLICATION: _____

_____

_____

_____

_____

MEMORY VERSE: Now faith is the substance of things hoped for, the evidence of things not seen.

Hebrews 11:1

⌁· DEVOTIONAL ·⌁

JAMES IS STRAIGHTFORWARD when it comes to exhorting believers to behave consistently, whether it comes to a recognition of our sinful inclinations, our lusts, our lack of prayer, our tendency to show favoritism to the well off in our congregations, or our failure to control our tongues. James exhorts us to resist the devil and humble ourselves in the sight of the Lord (James 4:7–10). He also calls on us to put our faith to work, to demonstrate our faith by lives of Christian service.

NEW TESTAMENT	OLD TESTAMENT
Monday. Hebrews 11:23–12:6	Job 5:17–21; Psalm 119:65–72
MEDITATION:	APPLICATION:
Tuesday. Hebrews 12:7–29	2 Samuel 24:8–15, 17–19, 25
MEDITATION:	APPLICATION:

Wednesday. Hebrews 13:1–25
MEDITATION: _____

_____
_____
_____
_____

Deuteronomy 10:12–21
APPLICATION: _____

_____
_____
_____
_____

Thursday. James 1:1–27
MEDITATION: _____

_____
_____
_____
_____

1 Kings 3:4–14
APPLICATION: _____

_____
_____
_____
_____

Friday. James 2:1–26
MEDITATION: _____

_____
_____
_____
_____

Obadiah 8, 10–15
APPLICATION: _____

_____
_____
_____
_____

Weekend. James 3:1–4:10
MEDITATION: _____

_____
_____
_____
_____

Psalm 141:1–4; Proverbs 10:11
APPLICATION: _____

_____
_____
_____
_____

MEMORY VERSES: Thus also faith by itself, if it does not have works, is dead. But someone will say, "You have faith, and I have works." Show me your faith without your works, and I will show you my faith by my works.

James 2:17–18

~· DEVOTIONAL ·~

THE APOSTLE PETER WROTE HIS first letter to churches in Asia
Minor that were undergoing, or would soon undergo, severe persecution.
He reminds them of their new birth by the Word, their special status as the
people of God, and the privilege they have to suffer for Christ. If suffering
must come, Peter is anxious that it be for the right reasons, because they are
Christians and not because of any misconduct on their part. He calls on
each person to be humble under the mighty hand of God and to resist the
devil, trusting God to be faithful (1 Peter 5:6–11).

NEW TESTAMENT	OLD TESTAMENT
Monday. James 4:11–5:20	Esther 4:9–16
MEDITATION:	APPLICATION:
Tuesday. 1 Peter 1:1–21	Isaiah 48:1–2, 8, 10
MEDITATION:	APPLICATION:

Wednesday. 1 Peter 1:22–2:17
MEDITATION: _____

Daniel 3:16–20, 26–29
APPLICATION: _____

Thursday. 1 Peter 2:18–3:12
MEDITATION: _____

Genesis 26:26–31
APPLICATION: _____

Friday. 1 Peter 3:13–4:11
MEDITATION: _____

Psalm 31:19–20, 23–24; 62:5–8
APPLICATION: _____

Weekend. 1 Peter 4:12–5:14
MEDITATION: _____

1 Kings 17:2–4, 6–16; Psalm 145:9
APPLICATION: _____

MEMORY VERSE: But sanctify the Lord God in your hearts, and always be ready to give a defense to everyone who asks you a reason for the hope that is in you, with meekness and fear.

1 Peter 3:15

⌣· DEVOTIONAL ·⌣

PETER, LIKE PAUL IN 2 TIMOTHY, is aware that his own death is impending (2 Peter 1:13–15ff). He presents a high view of the inspiration of Scripture (1:19–21), warning his readers against false teachers and their immoral lifestyle (2 Peter 2). He urges them not to be impatient about Christ's second coming, attributing any delay to God's desire to extend the day of salvation (quoting Paul on this, along with other Scriptures, 3:15–16). Peter prophesies the consumption of the current earth and skies in fire, and the appearance of a new heaven and earth (3:12–13). In light of the end of the world, we should be living godly lives (3:11).

NEW TESTAMENT	OLD TESTAMENT
Monday. 2 Peter 1:1–21	Proverbs 2:3–6; 1:1–5; 8:9–10
MEDITATION:	APPLICATION:
Tuesday. 2 Peter 2:1–22	Isaiah 56:9–12; Hosea 4:7–10
MEDITATION:	APPLICATION:

Wednesday. 2 Peter 3:1–18

MEDITATION: _____

_____

_____

_____

_____

Psalm 22:3–8; Isaiah 5:18–19

APPLICATION: _____

_____

_____

_____

_____

Thursday. 1 John 1:1–2:14

MEDITATION: _____

_____

_____

_____

_____

Isaiah 9:2; 42:6–7; Psalm 43:3–4

APPLICATION: _____

_____

_____

_____

_____

Friday. 1 John 2:15–3:10

MEDITATION: _____

_____

_____

_____

_____

Proverbs 28:13; Ezekiel 30

APPLICATION: _____

_____

_____

_____

_____

Weekend. 1 John 3:11–4:12

MEDITATION: _____

_____

_____

_____

_____

Zechariah 7:9–12; 2 Samuel 9:3–10

APPLICATION: _____

_____

_____

_____

_____

MEMORY VERSE: Therefore, since all these things will be dissolved, what manner of persons ought you to be in holy conduct and godliness . . . ?

2 Peter 3:11

⌒· DEVOTIONAL ·⌒

JOHN'S FIRST LETTER FOCUSES on those things that mark the children of God, those who are born again of His Spirit and in whom His Spirit dwells. They include a lifestyle of righteousness rather than sin, a love for fellow believers, a witness for Jesus Christ as the Son of God come in the flesh. And these are interrelated. We cannot claim to love God if we do not love our brother, or if we do not keep God's commandments. If we can affirm these marks and have Christ in us, we may know we have eternal life.

NEW TESTAMENT	OLD TESTAMENT
Monday. 1 John 4:13–5:21	Psalm 66:16–20; Jeremiah 42:1–3
MEDITATION:	APPLICATION:
Tuesday. 2 John 1–3	Deuteronomy 31:7–8
MEDITATION:	APPLICATION:

Wednesday. Jude 1–13

MEDITATION: _____

_____

_____

_____

_____

Psalm 50:10–23; Isaiah 13:6–11

APPLICATION: _____

_____

_____

_____

_____

Thursday. Jude 14–25

MEDITATION: _____

_____

_____

_____

_____

Jeremiah 14:13–16; 9:23–24

APPLICATION: _____

_____

_____

_____

_____

Friday. Revelation 1:1–20

MEDITATION: _____

_____

_____

_____

_____

Isaiah 48:12–13; 43:13; 44:6

APPLICATION: _____

_____

_____

_____

_____

Weekend. Revelation 2:1–17

MEDITATION: _____

_____

_____

_____

_____

Jeremiah 3:12; 2:1–9

APPLICATION: _____

_____

_____

_____

_____

MEMORY VERSE: These things I have written to you who believe in the name of the Son of God, that you may know that you have eternal life, and that you may continue to believe in the name of the Son of God.

1 John 5:13

⌒· DEVOTIONAL ·⌒

THE REVELATION OF JESUS CHRIST is full of imagery as well as prophecy of things to come. Jesus is portrayed as an awesome king sitting upon the throne of God. He is also portrayed as the Lamb who was slain and yet lives forevermore. John receives messages for the seven churches of Asia Minor, some of commendation and some of warning to repent. He also sees visions of heaven, of angels, of slain martyrs, and glimpses of future tribulation as one seal after another of the scroll is opened. Our God is an awesome God!

NEW TESTAMENT	OLD TESTAMENT
Monday. Revelation 2:18–3:6	Deuteronomy 10:12; 26:17–18
MEDITATION:	APPLICATION:
Tuesday. Revelation 3:7–4:5	Isaiah 22:22–25; Zephaniah 1:14–16
MEDITATION:	APPLICATION:

Wednesday. Revelation 4:6–6:2   Isaiah 6:1–8; Ezekiel 1:3–6
MEDITATION: _____   APPLICATION: _____

_____   _____

_____   _____

_____   _____

_____   _____

Thursday. Revelation 6:3–7:8   Nahum 1:2–6
MEDITATION: _____   APPLICATION: _____

_____   _____

_____   _____

_____   _____

_____   _____

Friday. Revelation 7:9–8:13   Isaiah 25:6–9; 51:6; 61:10
MEDITATION: _____   APPLICATION: _____

_____   _____

_____   _____

_____   _____

_____   _____

Weekend. Revelation 9:1–10:4   Joel 2:1–3, 6, 10–13
MEDITATION: _____   APPLICATION: _____

_____   _____

_____   _____

_____   _____

_____   _____

MEMORY VERSE: Behold, I stand at the door and knock. If anyone hears
My voice and opens the door, I will come in to him and dine with him, and
he with Me.

Revelation 3:20

⌣· DEVOTIONAL ·⌣

ONE CANNOT READ of the three and one-half years of tribulation on the earth, or of the beast that demands worship, or of the forcing of everyone to have the mark of the beast, the number of man which is 666, without shuddering. The picture of an angry Satan, cast out of heaven onto the earth, venting his wrath because his time is short, is fearsome. But more terrible are the vials of God's wrath poured out on the unrepentant. Unsaved people should indeed fear a God of judgment, and repent while there is time.

NEW TESTAMENT	OLD TESTAMENT
Monday. Revelation 10:5–11:14	Zechariah 4:11–14; Exodus 7:19–20
MEDITATION:	APPLICATION:
Tuesday. Revelation 11:15–12:12	Psalm 2:1–6; Daniel 7:13–18, 21–22
MEDITATION:	APPLICATION:

Wednesday. Revelation 12:13

MEDITATION: _____

_____

_____

_____

_____

Daniel 7:27; 11:29–35

APPLICATION: _____

_____

_____

_____

_____

Thursday. Revelation 14:1–20

MEDITATION: _____

_____

_____

_____

_____

Joel 3:12–13; Jeremiah 25:15–17, 26

APPLICATION: _____

_____

_____

_____

_____

Friday. Revelation 15:1–16:11

MEDITATION: _____

_____

_____

_____

_____

Deuteronomy 32:1–6, 15, 19–20

APPLICATION: _____

_____

_____

_____

_____

Weekend. Revelation 16:12–17:8

MEDITATION: _____

_____

_____

_____

_____

Ezekiel 13:8–13; 38:18–2

APPLICATION: _____

_____

_____

_____

_____

MEMORY VERSES: Then I saw another angel flying in the midst of heaven, having the everlasting gospel to preach to those who dwell on the earth—to every nation, tribe, tongue, and people—saying with a loud voice, "Fear God and give glory to Him, for the hour of His judgment has come; and worship Him who made heaven and earth, the sea and springs of water."

Revelation 14:6–7

⌁· DEVOTIONAL ·⌁

THE CLIMACTIC MOMENTS OF HUMAN HISTORY stagger the imagination. Christ's return in power and glory with those who are His own, the seeming threat of hostile armies under the command of Satan surrounding Jerusalem, the judgment seat of Christ when the books are opened, the New Jerusalem descending out of heaven, the unrepentant enemies of Christ cast into a lake of fire to suffer separation from God forever, the redeemed reigning with Christ in glory, make us cry out with John, "Even so, come, Lord Jesus" (Revelation 22:20)!

NEW TESTAMENT	OLD TESTAMENT
Monday. Revelation 17:9–18:10	Genesis 19:12–15; Jeremiah 51:6
MEDITATION: _____	APPLICATION: _____
_____	_____
_____	_____
_____	_____
Tuesday. Revelation 18:11–24	Jeremiah 51:25–26, 36–50
MEDITATION: _____	APPLICATION: _____
_____	_____
_____	_____
_____	_____

Wednesday. Revelation 19:1–16
MEDITATION: _____

Exodus 15:11–13, 17–18
APPLICATION: _____

_____
_____
_____
_____

_____
_____
_____
_____

Thursday. Revelation 19:17–20:15
MEDITATION: _____

Isaiah 24:21–22; 29:6–8
APPLICATION: _____

_____
_____
_____
_____

_____
_____
_____
_____

Friday. Revelation 21:1–27
MEDITATION: _____

Isaiah 65:17–19, 22
APPLICATION: _____

_____
_____
_____
_____

_____
_____
_____
_____

Weekend. Revelation 22:1–21
MEDITATION: _____

Isaiah 55:1–3; Psalm 46:4–5a
APPLICATION: _____

_____
_____
_____
_____

_____
_____
_____
_____

MEMORY VERSE: And God will wipe away every tear from their eyes; there shall be no more death, nor sorrow, nor crying. There shall be no more pain, for the former things have passed away.

Revelation 21:4